HOWLING
BEHIND
CEMENT
WALLS

A Healer's Journey

D1367283

LYNN STRAVECKY

HOWLING BEHIND CEMENT WALLS
Written by Lynn Stravecky
Editing: Erin Goodman
Design and Layout: George Riverón

© Lynn Stravecky, 2021
  www.lynnstravecky.com

First Edition, 2021

ISBN: 978-0-578-96342-6

TABLE OF CONTENTS

INTRODUCTION

I always teach my patients to start each day with a positive affirmation: "I am healthy, I am healed, I am loved."

Life is to be lived by overcoming and freeing yourself from painful addictions. This journey will allow for a deep evolution leading to transformation of your true self.

I always say "have a love affair with yourself every day and see what kind of sober man or woman you can be." I certainly did not know what that meant most of my life.

My moral compass was broken and I made up the rules as I went along. I thought life was supposed to be a safe place and no matter what choices I made I was supposed to be comfortable wherever I stand.

With time, I learned otherwise. Instead of feeling and facing life as an adult, I chose to self-medicate, this led me to the hard road of alcohol addiction. Only when I realized that it was ok to be imperfect and I had the power to turn my life around is when I began to see the light at the end of the tunnel. Awakening to my self-worth allowed me to connect with my universal source, which I chose to call the Divine.

Being a sacred healer and psychotherapist has allowed me to personally evolve and be a beacon of light for thousands of others. My approach to life, sobriety and manifestation is simple; water the plant on a daily basis (self-care) and the path you desire will flourish.

My spiritual path has been one that continues to grow and I treasure all the participants and pains thus far. All of the players along the way have been master teachers and helped me create the person and life I embrace today. One of grace, joy and dignity.

Who's to say when the real journey to enlightenment begins? Mine may have begun during many wake up calls during my life. Or possibly, it was during one of the darkest moments when I encountered the wolf.

The decisions we make can take a split second and be life chang-ing. I am so grateful I followed my intuition to become a spiritual healer and found the courage to get sober. Facing life on life's terms has been a gift I hold dear. These two decisions have significantly changed me and the way I help others in my private practice as a holistic psychotherapist.

Everyone in my life has served a purpose. Whether they hurt me or appreciate me. They have helped me grow and become the person I am becoming.

I share my story with the intention it serves as a helping hand to those who seek freedom from the bondage of addiction.

Be the change you want to be and feel free to live a beautiful life!

Love, Light, and Awakening
LYNN STRAVECKY

PROLOGUE

My name is Lynn Ann Mary Stravecky. I was born in Bridgeport, Connecticut, the second-oldest child of four. I always felt different from my brother and sisters, mainly because I was never clear on my place at home. I seemed to be the one always getting into trouble. I felt like I was the only one expected to do everything right. Sharing deep emotions was not something taught to either of my parents, nor did they encourage that trait in me. They did their best, and they tried to instill in me their strong values and beliefs about life, religion, and respect. Much of which I seemed to disagree with.

I had always had a somewhat defiant nature, I guess that's why I often found myself being daring and careless, feeling invincible. Looking back at those days, I can see how my behavior was but a cry for help that went unheard. With time, my attention-seeking behavior and reckless ways led me to spend time with the wrong crowds, who would eventually introduce me to drugs and alcohol. It didn't take long for me to get swirled away into the ruthless world of addiction.

Many years later, I woke up and looked out my bedroom window feeling grateful for the blessing of seeing how the sun shone differently before my eyes. I took that opportunity to look back at my life and realized that I was not particularly proud of anything I had done up until that day. I was lost between codependency and alcohol and a voice from within whispered, *you're wasting your potential and life*. From that day forward, I began my search for sobriety, and in the process, I learned that I had to set aside any pride and guilt. I faced my past mistakes, and with that came cleaning my side of the street. I had to stop feeling sorry for myself since I was the only one who'd put myself where I was.

Being honest with yourself is the key to opening doors that lead to the complex journey of recovery. Such a path has been a rocky one for me. There are two main mistakes that anyone seeking sobriety can make: First, being *dishonest* about your own reality, and second, depriving yourself of the gift of sobriety by not fully working through your recovery.

Today I am proud to have accomplished twelve years of sobriety. During my sobriety I found the ability to fall in love with myself. Along the way I have become a successful psychotherapist, dynamic guest speaker, and sacred healer. Most importantly, I am a mother of two amazing young adults, who are full of energy, potential, and most significantly, of my love.

Through my work as a psychotherapist and Sacred Healer I help hundreds of people who battle with addiction, life-changing events, and other issues. Helping them helps me stay grounded and grateful on a daily basis.

My transformation did not happen overnight nor did it come easy. I like to think everything I went through was perfectly orchestrated in order for me to be where I am, with the story I find worth telling you today.

I hope that my story can inspire you to seek and find the power that I found within myself for an amazing life. You deserve to give yourself the chance to know and see what kind of sober person you were meant to be.

Some names in this story have been changed to respect privacy. All events are true.

Victimization solves nothing.

*I have not ceased
being fearful,
but I have ceased
to let fear control me.*
ERICA JONG

MY BEGINNING

I was only a few months shy of my high school graduation at Bunnell High School in the small town of Stratford, Connecticut. Like most girls at that age, I, too, was excitedly planning a great senior prom night with my boyfriend, then graduation parties, and soon after I would be on my way to college.

One morning I was having breakfast at the kitchen table across from my brother, Tim. We were rushing because I had woken up a few minutes late. I tended to gulp down my first meal before I would run out just in time to catch the bus to school.

"What's wrong with you?" Tim asked as I lifted a spoonful of cereal to my mouth. I glanced at him annoyed by his inflection.

"Hmm?" I shrugged. At that moment, I put the cereal into my mouth and felt the milk drip down my chin. I took another spoonful, thinking it happened because I was in too much of a rush. This time the milk and cereal dribbled down the side of my mouth onto my shirt and the table. I panicked.

"Mom!" I let out a hysterical cry. My mother was getting ready for work and ignored my calling. She was used to hearing my complaints or my brothers' first thing in the morning. I called out again with a trembling voice and tears streaming down my face. I ran out of the kitchen and we bumped into each other in the hallway. I looked at her with big eyes, now crying. She stared at me horrified. The right side of my face was completely paralyzed.

Mom ran back to the bedroom and called my dad at work. "Her face looks strange!" she said loudly. He couldn't understand. "She can't talk!" my mother insisted. I didn't hear his reaction but I assumed that he suggested my mother take me to our family doctor, because she grabbed her purse and cigarettes, and rushed me to the car. We didn't exchange words on the way to the clinic and both of us were scared and in shock.

The doctor's office was near our home in Stratford and the ride was a short one. Mom parked abruptly and walked out of the car with her cigarette in hand. I followed her with my legs shaking from nerves. I didn't know what was wrong with me or what to expect.

We walked inside the doctor's office and I went straight to sit in a corner while trying to hide my face with my hoodie. The doctor motioned us into his office. He was flustered at the sight of me and explained that he couldn't give us a precise diagnosis because I would need to be seen by a neurologist. The doctor referred my case to someone he knew and Mom didn't waste a minute driving me to his office.

The neurologist saw me immediately. Back then, medical technology was not as advanced and there was no magnetic resonance imaging (MRI) available. The neurologist diagnosed me with Bell's palsy, a condition that causes a temporary paralysis of the facial muscles, causing one side of the face to droop or become stiff. He prescribed an intense regime of physical therapy along with steroids, electrical stimulation for the affected area, and facial exercises that he encouraged me to practice at home daily.

That experience shattered all the excitement and expectation I had for high school graduation and prom. Word had spread quickly at school and I was indignant, mainly because I was ashamed of my appearance. My friends at school heard about it and insisted on coming over but I was reluctant to see anyone at first. I had been the captain for the High Steppers team at my school, which was like cheerleaders—we performed dance routines at football half times, competitions, and some assembly events. I felt like a big sister to all twenty-four girls on our team and they all considered me a good leader. Now, their much-admired leader didn't want to see them or anyone else, and felt safe isolated in her bedroom. Weeks into my treatment I came to terms with the fact that my face may never be the same, and depression sank in.

This all seemed surreal. Just the week before I was on top of the world performing our dance routines on the football field at half time with the step team. I recall it had been a very cold and windy day, which left little protection with our tiny outfits. Shortly thereafter, my right ear started to ache, which I paid no mind to and thought it may be the beginning of a cold brought on by the weather.

I am in the second row, fourth from left.

Graduation Day
Bunnell High School, Stratford, CT

Once I realized that I couldn't be a recluse forever, I reluctantly started to return phone calls and spent time with my best friend when she came to my house to see me. She was also on the High Steppers team and quickly filled me in all the gossip at school. She was loving and cheerful and helped me feel connected to my school days for the first time in weeks. We talked and talked and then I noticed how hard she was trying to make me laugh before breaking the news.

"I don't know how to tell you this," she said. "Jerry is going to the prom with Tina."

Jerry and I hadn't seen each other in weeks. He had spoken to my mother the same night I suffered facial paralysis and only called me twice after that. He didn't bother to send me flowers or check on me. Nevertheless, when my best friend told me that he was going to the prom with someone else, I couldn't help but feel crushed. She read my demeanor and continued gently.

"They've been going out for the past few weeks, I thought you needed to know," she said.

Jerry was considered the best-looking guy in school. He was tall, blue-eyed, and blond, the popular captain of the football team. We had dated for two years and I was proud to say he was my high school sweetheart. My parents liked him and perhaps that's why we were puzzled at his abrupt absence during my recovery. He hadn't stopped by my house to see me, not even once. Initially, I knew his indifference was completely out of character but when I mentioned it to my mother; she attributed his lack of interest to poor coping skills or immaturity. My father insisted that he was only taking time away in an effort to respect my process and space.

I felt that my identity was completely gone. I didn't know what to think about Jerry, though I must admit I was quite relieved he didn't see my disfigured face.

When my best friend left, I stayed in my room and cried for hours before going to bed. Because the right side was paralyzed, I couldn't close my eye. I was forced to tape my right eye shut to prevent it from drying out. Even crying was a difficult task. For the 17-year-old girl I was, the world seemed to crumble before me.

After that night, I went into hermit mode and didn't want to see anyone for the next few weeks.

On the night of the senior prom, three months later, I chose to go back to my part-time job at a small local restaurant called Arthur Treacher's Fish & Chips. I felt less lonely there because I felt needed and appreciated by my co-workers, they were a great support. Working like everyone else in the same space gave me a strong sense of normalcy. I became aware that if I didn't talk, I actually appeared normal, with no facial paralysis. That night was excruciatingly painful.

Days after the prom, I heard that my ex-boyfriend had taken his new girlfriend out that night and joined our group of friends. I felt completely left out. I had been replaced, just like that. My girlfriends were supportive and encouraged me to go out, and after the spring I would join them at the movies, but they all knew that I preferred having them over at my house to avoid being out in public.

Before my facial paralysis, Mom was opposed to my friends coming over and stressed the fact that our house was no social club. After my paralysis, her attitude shifted completely. Not only would she allow my friends to come over to see me whenever I wanted, but she would encourage it. Little did she know the girls showed up at our doorstep with angelic smiles before dropping their arsenal of pills, alcohol, Quaaludes, or marijuana at my bedside minutes later.

Other than their drinking and smoking habits, my parents were pretty old-fashioned. They dragged us to mass at church every Sunday, and it was mandatory for us to attend weekly confession. I absolutely detested these rituals, but I knew better than to resist.

I had never felt guilty about sneaking and hiding what I considered experimental treats. With time the treats became self-destructive vices. I thought that the church-going was a tradition for my parents, not a redeeming quality of their lifestyle. In all honesty, the trips to church did nothing to make me feel better or heal my crushed self-esteem. For me, self-medicating with intoxicating substances was more effective than a Sunday mass or a half-hour confession. My parents never took the time to sit with me and talk about my feelings or my inferiority complex due to my condition, and I guess that on a subconscious level I resented them for that. I also had a lot of anger about how my senior year ended.

Summer finally arrived, and my siblings and I were never too excited to cram together in the back of my dad's Station Wagon on our way to some camping site. My parents were hard-working people and made just enough to get by, so camping was about all they could afford. My last summer vacation with the family before leaving for college came after graduation. We were all happy to see how much my face had nearly fully recovered from the paralysis (except when I drank or smoked marijuana...).

I was beginning to feel myself again, and was looking forward to leaving the house and heading to college. I had dreams of attending the University of Connecticut or any other large state university; but my parents insisted I attended a women's college. Eventually, I complied and enrolled in the now-closed Hartford College for Women. It was a very small campus compared to most colleges, and I was not particularly fond of the idea. However, I had become an expert on dealing with my frustrations. Comfort was only a joint and a drink away.

OFF TO COLLEGE

I was eager to leave my small hometown, and hopeful to embrace the freedom that independence brings. College in Harford was an hour away from home, yet to me it wasn't far enough.

I couldn't wrap my head around having fun at an all-women's school. Nevertheless, I gave in to my parents' supplications and by the time moving day came around, I was thrilled. My stuff had been packed for the past six weeks and I couldn't wait to leave. Dad and Mom packed everything into their old Station Wagon and drove me over to campus. I had a few days to settle in before classes began.

As we drove through the gate, I glanced at the area looking at the layout of the two-story buildings forming a close circle. I thought it looked more like a small condominium subdivision than student dorms.

We parked in front of one of the buildings and double-checked the address on my envelope before I rushed to the door, dragging my old suitcase. Mom and Dad carried my things from the car trunk to the front door. Mom had the key and the moment she opened the door, I made sure I was first to walk in. My eyes scanned the layout and I was in awe at the spacious place. Each unit had four bedrooms, two upstairs and two downstairs, with a kitchen, living room, and two bathrooms. Coming from my tiny bedroom in the attic, the space alone was paradise to me. I didn't care about sharing my space with strangers—it was my own apartment and roommates didn't matter, I could finally breathe some freedom.

"Let me set this up for you," said Mom, walking behind me while she carried a box filled to the brim with sheets and towels. I walked straight to my bedroom on the first floor. Bedrooms had been assigned in advance and it was marked on the layout they had handed my mother along with the keys.

Mom unpacked the box, placing my belongings in a small walk-in closet.

"I've got it!" I said, and took the folded sheets from her. I wanted to enjoy the whole process by myself and I wanted them to leave as quickly as possible.

I expressed my gratitude, hugged them good-bye, and assured them that I would behave. They suspected that I would enjoy my new place and since I was in an all-girls' environment, they trusted I'd be okay.

The tight leash my parents kept me on had become unbearable, and my relationship with my sister was not one I would miss. I walked them outside to the parking lot. As soon as their car was gone, I sat by the window and lit a cigarette. To my immature mind, I truly was under the impression that toxic habits were a sign of independence. Either way, it was quite a relief to start a new phase in my life away from my past.

Walking out of my room, I bumped into one of my future roommates.

"Hi!" I said enthusiastically.

"I'm Rosemary," she replied, shaking my hand politely. By the look on her face I could tell she was annoyed by the smoke.

"Do you mind?" I asked.

"I don't smoke, but I don't mind," she said, and walked straight to the kitchen to unload the groceries.

That night I had a chance to meet our other two roommates, Pat and Linda. That first night, we all went to the cafeteria and got to know each other a little. I knew at a glance that in the house where I had just found my newly acquired independence, my presence would be looked down upon as less conventional. I saw clearly that I had nothing in common with my college roommates. Therefore, I took it upon myself to survey each building in search of new roommates that would complement my reckless lifestyle.

And soon enough, I found Cindy, Jennifer, and Joan. Luckily, the college allowed me to change housing. My new family and I bonded like sorority sisters and we were always there to cover for each other.

My parents had helped me through the process of getting into college but they couldn't afford to pay my way. I had no choice but to get by with student loans, babysitting, and eventually working in the main kitchen on a work-study program. This was not the norm in this Hartford College environment. Most of the girls came from wealthy families and seemed to live relatively close by. Most of their parents paid their way. They had their own cars on campus and personal phones in their rooms, too. Certainly, they were not working in the kitchen with the big Jamaican cook, whom I grew to love like a grandmother. She was kind and loving, just what I needed to feel comforted away from home.

My new roommates and I would go out almost nightly, or gather to smoke bongs, drink beer, and eat pizza. Until this day, I still wonder how I passed from one semester to the next with all the pot, bong smoking, and drinking that went on.

During my college days I was thrilled to develop a close relationship with my brother Tim, who was attending Boston University.

Back at home growing up, Tim and I couldn't tolerate each other. We always seemed at odds, tattling on each other to our mother, who encouraged this behavior, giving us more attention and praise. Surprisingly, the day came when we found communality in toxic habits, and we started to bond. Sometimes I would hitch-hike from Hartford to Boston just to spend the weekend with Tim. I embraced this newfound closeness. I would go to the highway, usually very stoned, with a "Going to Boston" sign, and somebody would always give me a ride. Living on the edge was part of my nature.

Sometimes when I went to visit Tim, we would discuss our upbringing while drinking and smoking. I would bring up certain incidents, like how I got beat with the belt or always screamed at by our mother. Tim tried to convince me that I always got in trouble because I "looked for it." Tim had not always been the warm nurturing older brother I would have liked. But as the only other pack member that I was bonding with, I gladly took what I could from him. I also liked the idea of having a "big brother," and bonding over toxic habits was better than nothing, I thought.

By the end of my freshman year in college, my drinking had escalated from twice a week to four times a week. The fact that I managed to earn an Associate's Degree in Liberal Arts while drugging and drinking regularly is beyond me. By the time I went back home I had put on twenty pounds from alcohol and junk food but I didn't care, because I had tasted freedom.

The idea of going back to college after I completed my Associate's Degree was repelling. I struggled thinking that I couldn't retain any information. The idea that perhaps the fact that I was taking drugs and alcohol on a daily basis had a big impact in that matter never occurred to me then—I just thought I was academically challenged.

So, I decided to quit studying and go to work. It was time to head back to Stratford and to my parents' attic, which would prove difficult. The reality was that I had been living in total freedom for two years, partying late at night and sleeping whenever I wanted. I made things work in college but I was fully aware that the lifestyle I was accustomed to would not fly at home. House rules meant getting home early every night.

My parents never cared to talk to us kids about dating or sex, so I learned about intimate interactions from my own mistakes and experiences. Going off to college was like "Catholic Girls Gone Wild" for me.

Mom and Dad still saw me as the high school girl I once was, and not like the young woman I had become. They restricted me from everything I had gotten used to, and all the old rules remained, including lights out by 10 p.m. Of course I was not on board with any of this. A request to have a phone in my room and a lock on my door was denied. Moving back home was a new transition for me and quite challenging. How could I go back to sneaking around, trying to hide my drinking and destructive lifestyle? It was clear I had to gain my independence back, at any cost.

One of the first things I knew I had to do to gain some kind of freedom was to find a job. I had no skills but I was desperate for money. I got a part-time job as a waitress at a venue for weddings and parties down the street from my parents' house. My enthusiasm was short-lived since I quickly got fired for getting drunk on the job at a New Year's Eve party and dancing with the guests. I thought it would be fun to do some shots with the people celebrating. On top of it, the owner was a good friend of my parents and they were devastated when he told them what I did. I quit many other low-paying jobs after that.

Time went on and my parents became desperate for me to get a job and start to have some kind of a normal adult life. Mom asked an uncle who worked in one of the largest factories in Stratford if he could get me a job. He was kind enough to offer to hire me as his secretary. Poor guy had no idea what train was about to hit him.

MICHAEL, THE OLDER MAN

I detested authority and I wasn't fond of working, either. I had no skills as a secretary, nor did I really want to learn. Back in the day, I was under the impression that secretaries were treated as second-class citizens, and I certainly wasn't going to succumb to the usual "Get me coffee... make me copies... take shorthand...." I detested the idea of that job, but it was part of the plan to become independent.

As an employee, I made many mistakes and socialized more than I worked. Or I came in hungover and took a nap in the ladies' room when I could. I was 21 years old. Without my parents' emotional support, I felt like a lost soul. My poor uncle had such good intentions and fell prey to my instability and recklessness when he offered to give me a job. I am very grateful to him to this day, as that helped me gain some skills and experience, and tamed some of my unprofessionalism.

One day, as I left my desk ready to break for lunch, I bumped into a co-worker. Periodically, Michael and I had chatted and made small talk, but for some reason that afternoon was different. We were in the break room, eating from the big pizza pie that our boss would usually get for the team on Fridays. He asked me if I played racquetball. I had thought of getting into sports, mainly to get in shape if only to look better in a pair of jeans (being health-conscious was nowhere on my radar at that time). I told him I didn't play but I'd love to learn, and that conversation led us to our first date.

Michael was 15 years older than I was, and I found that intriguing. We became drinking buddies and though he was the heavier drinker, eventually I would catch up. I was impressed by the fact that he lived alone in his own studio apartment (he had just gone through a divorce). My perception of good living was so distorted that I was positively impressed to know that he kept an abundant supply of marijuana, cocaine, alcohol, and cigarettes at his place, which was heaven for me compared to my room in the attic. Being with an older man was exciting for me and a distraction to my humdrum life.

When I introduced Michael to my parents they were hesitant at first but eventually they warmed up to him. He was an unusual drug user, now that I think back. He did sports, played baseball, was a professional engineer, and had a nice little apartment. All that while remaining functional at work. His reality lured me into thinking that I could manage the same. His example only fed my delusion into thinking that drinking and drugging was a normal part of anyone's lifestyle.

Michael and I dated for two years. While he was head-over-heels for me, with time my interest dissipated and I was less thrilled about him with each passing day. He was tall and strong, and always wore a baseball hat—the moment he removed it, he would expose his bald head and the few remaining grey hairs. I tried not to go out in public with him and preferred the isolation we both enjoyed by getting high at his place when I stayed the night. My parents thought that most weekends I was at some girlfriend's house. The reality was that anything looked and felt amazing for me as long as it was far away from my little room in the attic and my parents' constant hovering and rules.

Michael marked the beginning of the end for me. My world with him encouraged a lifestyle of delusion, lying, and self-destruction, leading to more bad decisions and self-harm. It was a cold morning, snowing lightly. I had slept at my parents' house the night before and asked Dad to let me borrow his car to go over to Michael's place in the morning. We had plans to go skiing in Vermont that day. I had keys to his place, so I didn't need to call him to announce myself. I walked in the door of his studio apartment at around 6 a.m. and found him in the bathroom, crouched over the toilet vomiting like a fraternity boy after a wild night of partying. For the first time, I felt disgusted. I had vomited many times myself, even peed on the bed once when I was too intoxicated to realize I needed to go to the bathroom. But him? *How low!* He was much older and I thought he was invincible. It was then that I came to terms that Michael was just another ordinary man and I started to lose respect for him. The idea of being shacked up in some old guy's studio apartment while drinking and drugging began to lose its charm. Needless to say, we never made it to Vermont that morning.

Living in my parents' house had become more difficult for all of us. One night after being with a friend and falling asleep at his place, I arrived home at 4 a.m. Dad was standing in the living room waiting and Mom hovered behind him.

Early that morning, they gave me an ultimatum: live by their rules or leave. So, being the rebel I was, I chose to leave, right then and there. Dad followed me to my room and watched me pack my things. I didn't know where to go and ended up at a girlfriend's house, knocking on her bedroom window. That arrangement only lasted about two weeks. I eventually crawled back home and, per usual, we didn't discuss any of this and life returned to what it had been. No discussions, no pep talk, no guidance, nothing—only the constant sick feeling in my gut and sense of failure as their daughter.

I truly struggled being back home under stern rules again, and neither my parents nor I were happy. It was a challenging time for all of us. My drug use and drinking became fiercer and more frequent after I returned home. I totaled a car one night and got stopped by a local cop for speeding on another occasion. Both times no breathalyzer was given, and nobody knew I was drunk. Or, if they did suspect, my small-town police officers looked the other way and marched me home. I desperately needed a way out.

JOHNNY, MR. TOXIC

Shortly after the incident with Michael, I received an offer to work in a different factory in Stratford. Even though it was yet another secretary position, this one had a different title: Administrative Assistant. The title sounded uplifting and the pay was better. I started to distance myself from Michael.

Sometime during the first week at my new job, I was at my desk when I sensed someone staring at me. As I looked up, I noticed a cute guy with piercing green eyes watching me. Little did I know, those eyes belonged to the devil himself.

As a lost young woman with a broken compass, his attention pulled me in like a northern star. Johnny worked next to me for a different department and after only a few days of interaction, any feelings left from my two-year relationship with Michael dissipated like smoke. I didn't break up with Michael right away, but he noticed I was emotionally absent. I was totally smitten with my new guy.

Johnny was six years older than me—black hair and a mustache, and a lot better looking than Michael. He smoked cigarettes and drank like a fish, but he didn't do drugs, which helped keep me away from them, too.

I wasn't thrilled with my new job, but somehow waking up to the expectation of running into Johnny made my mornings more tolerable. From the moment we met, Johnny and I had a kind of magnetism that I had never experienced, and he even made me forget how much I had enjoyed getting high way back when. This new relationship made me realize how delightful it was to go out with someone in my age range. I was no longer embarrassed of introducing my boyfriend to my friends... until much later.

After a month of hiding my double life from Michael, I had to come clean. The breakup came as a surprise to him and he was devastated. Nevertheless, I carried on feeling as if I had just cut the cord that had kept me connected to a false sense of independence.

One day after work I invited Johnny to join me for a jog at the high school track near my parents' house. He seemed delighted and we went for an hour jog. By the time we came back to my parents' house, they were home from work. Johnny and I were still sweaty, and instead of water I made it a point to offer him a beer. We were sitting on the front porch with a six-pack when my father walked out.

"What's this?" he asked.

"What's what?" I answered. He was obviously disturbed. Drinking beer after an hour jog was not his idea of wrapping up a workout. That was the first time he and Mom met Johnny, and they were not impressed.

Johnny and I dated for a few months. Unlike Michael, Johnny had a nice condo, a new car, and apart from his heavy drinking he had a pretty decent lifestyle. I was mesmerized by this new man in my life, and felt like I had just won the jackpot. My friends had a different take and were not thrilled, since I was spending less and less time with them. They all thought we were moving too fast and they were not fond of this new guy at all.

Shortly after we started dating, Johnny began to pressure me into staying over at his place more often. By then I was an expert at lying to my parents. Little by little I felt more isolated from friends and family. Johnny was extremely jealous of anyone who took a minute of my time from him. Even my talking on the phone with Tim infuriated him. I had no idea of the death trap I was walking into.

Tim and I had grown closer after our times in college, and he expressed his concern about Johnny's possessiveness. Unfortunately, I attributed his attitude to his deep love for me. I felt protected. My crushed self-esteem wouldn't let me see otherwise. My own family had grave concerns and didn't care for him either.

Eight months had passed when Johnny blew me away with unexpected news. He had been offered an opportunity with our company, but it required relocating to Brazil. We were at his place having drinks and watching TV when he broke the news.

"I think I'll be taking the offer to go work in Brazil," he said. I looked at him puzzled.

"What do you mean? For how long?" I asked.

"Two to five years," he said nonchalantly and walked to the kitchen. I followed him into the kitchen, indignant.

"When were you planning to tell me?"

"I just did," he answered with a cool stare. He suggested that I go with him. I told him I couldn't. There was no way my parents would approve of it. We weren't married and despite my non-conventional lifestyle, I couldn't just pick up and run away to some other country with a guy. Besides, I had my own income and health insurance for protection.

Johnny knew that my parents were devout Catholics, so he did what he had to: he asked my hand in marriage. Soon into our relationship I would learn just how manipulative and sick he could be to get his way and control me. At that age, I was completely naive about narcissism or the damage that would come to me.

At that time, I was thrilled and accepted. Mom wasn't happy with the idea and insisted that I was making a huge mistake. I met Johnny's mother shortly after we got engaged. The moment Johnny stood up from the table his mother took the opportunity to warn me: "Please, don't marry my son. You're such a sweet girl." Those were the words that came out of his own mother's mouth. I smiled, thinking she was just a typical overprotective future mother-in-law.

My parents insisted that we get married in the church next door to our house, and so we did. Even though neither of us could care less about the church, we knew that they were paying for our wedding and that is how it would be.

It was clear to me on our wedding day as I entered the church that my family was completely against it. My dad glanced at me before we walked down the aisle.

"Are you sure, honey?" he asked me in a whisper. I smiled and nodded but he could see the fear in my eyes.

I chose not to drink at the reception. Johnny drank enough for both of us. I believe he was even drunk at the altar.

After the reception and once we made our way back to the apartment, I had a few drinks just to catch up with him. We argued about his attitude during the reception, which had been appalling. He didn't behave like a proper groom and wouldn't speak to the guests or thank them. I was young and embarrassed and didn't know what to do. He insisted I was being paranoid.

We drank until the wee hours and almost missed our flight to our honeymoon in Jamaica. The taxi had arrived earlier than expected and awakened us with his persistent calls. The first day of my life married to this man should have been a red flag about what was in store for me—we both woke up with severe hangovers and unprepared for our flight. Nevertheless, I ignored the warning signs.

My idea of a romantic honeymoon was far from our reality. Johnny and I spent most of our honeymoon drinking and fighting over trivial things. His abusive side emerged with a vengeance. Within a short time span the emotional abuse and fighting dynamics became commonplace.

Johnny left to Brazil to get settled and start his new assignment. I agreed to join him later and spent the next few days packing our things. The night before my flight I spent most of the late afternoon hours sitting at the kitchen table, talking to my parents. My father tried to convince me not to go, expressing grave concerns about my life with Johnny and my safety. And when I told my mother that I would be flying to Brazil all by myself she kept quiet. I knew that look: she was petrified for me.

The next day I was on the first flight to São Paulo. It was then I realized I may have made a huge mistake. I had mixed feelings about my new adventure. Looking back, I don't think I was clear about the serious commitment I had gotten myself into. I doubted myself often but I would never have admitted to it.

The trip to Brazil was pleasant and I slept for most of the eight-hour flight from Miami. When we finally landed, I watched the flight attendant open the aircraft's main door while the land crew dragged the metal staircase for the passengers to disembark the plane. Once on the ground, a shuttle took us over to Immigration. Fear started to settle into this small-time girl from Stratford, Connecticut.

It was almost an hour before I was able to pick up my luggage and hop on a smaller plane that would take me to Belém, a small town somewhere between civilization and the Amazon River, where Johnny was stationed. There were less than twenty passengers on this flight, so everything went much smoother upon landing. After getting the attention of a young baggage handler who placed all my suitcases neatly on a cart, I exited and scanned the area outside the gate. There were metal barriers and people waved their arms while shouting names and greetings in Portuguese, looking to get the attention of some friend or family member. I heard my name from a distance—it was Johnny. He was there, at the end of the line waving at me with a big smile. For the first time in a long time, I felt butterflies in my stomach. I wasn't sure if the feeling was one of happy excitement or perhaps one of fear.

We hugged and he introduced me to our driver. Along the way, I cringed at the sight of naked children running barefoot over mud and debris, amongst garbage and wild dogs, abandoned cars, and dead animals. Small grass or mud huts on the side of the road and people begging and running after our car. The ride was less than an hour and we finally made it to the gated community that was home to over one hundred American expat families. It was a world away from its surroundings, where shacks with tin roofs prevailed, and concrete roads and paved streets were non-existent.

Belém, the capital of the state of Pará,
is a port city and gateway to Brazil's lower Amazon region.

BRAZIL

The inside of our home—what was to be my prison for the next two years—was immense, with marble floors and fully furnished for royalty. Johnny was excited and oblivious to my inner turmoil. Nonetheless, I tried to put on a happy "new bride" face and play the role.

Settling in was a daunting task, not just with the cultural differences, and of course, everything, including TV, was in Portuguese. There were no cell phones at that time to communicate with anybody. Johnny had work to attend to at his job and he left me alone shortly after I arrived, which left me feelng helpless and frightened. Luckily, Johnny had stocked the house with rum, which seemed to be my constant from that day forward. I was scared, regretful and lonely all the time.

During my first year in Brazil I spent most days and nights at home in isolation. Not knowing how to fill my free time, coupled with the anxiety of living in a different culture, I drank myself to sleep almost nightly. I was terrified to drive and be away from the security and comfort of our gated community. I eventually ventured out and met some of the other expats, who were all older than me. But, they all loved to drink and I knew we would be good friends.

Shortly after living in seclusion, I found a local to teach me Portuguese, which was not easy for me. I loved animals and one day Johnny surprised me with a German Shepherd puppy, Amanda. She became my partner, friend, protector and constant companion. I don't know how I would have survived without her. I missed my brother, my parents and my friends. I even missed my small room in the attic.

My drinking had gotten so bad that the mental obsession for alcohol had enslaved me every night, when I would drink myself to the point of blacking out. This was the only way I knew how to cope. I told myself that I didn't have a drinking problem because I never drank during the daytime. I was under the impression that an alcoholic usually wakes up craving a beer in the morning or a Bloody Mary. Since that was not my case, I was fine. I cared little to socialize with anyone other than Johnny. I was young, naïve, and a hostage in my new world.

We traveled back home to Connecticut for Christmas that first year. I had been drinking so much that I was unrecognizable to my family and my father didn't waste time letting me know. I noticed my mother's sadness in her eyes. She hugged me and I could sense her pain. I was confused, thinking that their lack of enthusiasm didn't make sense. They should've been happy to see me, but instead, what was supposed to be a joyous moment felt more like a funeral. The truth was that my mother was horrified at how I had become bloated from excess drinking and my disheveled appearance. I had put on over twenty pounds and my swollen eyes were hidden by my puffy cheeks. I looked far older than my 23 years.

While at my parents' that Christmas, I experienced the first self-doubt about my condition. I was painting my nails next to my little sister at the kitchen table. She was staring at me and I could sense it.

"What?" I asked defensively.

"Why are your hands shaking so much?" she asked.

I preferred to say that I had low blood sugar, though deep inside I knew that maybe alcohol had something to do with it. Being at home, I realized that I was constantly ashamed about who I had become.

Johnny and I stayed over at his mother's house, where we didn't do much other than drink and fight, which had become our new normal. The night after Christmas we had such a blowout confrontation that I got in our rental car and drove away. The only thing I remember is waking up at my sister's house. Today I say that I made it there safely by the grace of God.

No other disastrous events faced us during our vacation and when the day came as I reluctantly re-packed our things, I wasn't thrilled about going back to Brazil. We said our goodbyes and got in the rental car. I waved goodbye to Mom as we drove away; she was in the doorway waving back with a drawn look on her face. I knew she was sad. I started to cry and Johnny asked me, "What's wrong?"

"Nothing," I said.

It was much easier to attribute my deep sadness to memories from childhood than it was to express how much I hated living in another country.

Shortly after we returned to Brazil, I found a job as an English teacher. That responsibility saved me from nightly drunken stupors, since I had to be up early and fresh for class during the weekdays. The ladies in the neighborhood also encouraged me to run for president of the Newcomers Club of Belém. I did so reluctantly and I got the position. These two commitments gave me some sense of purpose and sanity while I was there.

I did, however, make sure to catch up on my destructive drinking habits during the weekends—at that point I would still drink myself to the point of blacking out. Little by little it had come to that, and I could only ever remember my first drink and never the last one.

Those days I lived for two things: my job as a teacher and reckless drinking. Johnny was distant, emotionally absent, and what started as a normal conversation would end up as a confrontation. I now know he was a classic narcissist gas-lighter. He seemed to enjoy constantly arguing and he blamed me for everything. My frustration only led me to isolate further with each passing day. I thought, *What a mistake I've made. Why did I marry this horrible man?* I was young, weak, and too embarrassed to tell anyone how much I regretted my marriage. I didn't see how I could reinvent myself while destroying my parents' expectations. Growing up, my parents had been emotionally absent, physically and emotionally abusive. Mom encouraged rivalry among us siblings and my parents argued often. But in our family, marriage was a one-time, forever event. I wanted to believe in the perfect home and ideal marriage and I obsessed over making Johnny happy enough to portray the perfect image as a couple. I was so consumed in pleasing everyone else that I had forgotten about myself. Codependency had now stolen any self-esteem I had left. I was slowly disappearing.

Another day after the market Johnny and I ventured out to the main streets on our own. On that day we found a small boy selling tiny baby monkeys. Of course I had to have one, which we bought for about one US dollar. I brought him home, named him Miko and nursed him daily with a small bottle. Until he was stronger, I would put him in my top pocket of a shirt or in my sock to keep him warm and safe next to my skin. Once he was grown a bit I moved him to a cage in the home. I loved my animals. I eventually bought a couple of large blue and gold Macaws, which were bred in captivity and became my babies, too. This small menagerie kept me going during the days I was alone. I learned enough Portuguese to communicate a bit and eventually felt secure enough to venture out on my own. I went to a spa frequently and got treatments for next to nothing. That was how I passed my days.

Then one day Johnny came home from work earlier than usual one morning. "We're going back to the States!" he said excitedly. I felt like someone had taken a sack of bricks off of my shoulders.

My isolation and heavy drinking had drained the life out of me and I really believed that the problem was that I'd been living elsewhere, far from my culture. I told myself that once back to the States, everything would change for the better.

Only weeks before moving back to the States, we found out that Johnny was being transferred to Miami, and I was thrilled to know we were moving to an exciting city versus a boring old town in Connecticut. For the first time in two years I felt a sense of purpose and excitement and the misery of excess drinking in isolation would be a thing of the past. *Things will be different in Miami, everything will change,* I convinced myself.

My only acquaintances in Brazil had been other expats, all much older than I and I had little in common with them. I did make one friend, Melike. She was from Turkey and her husband was Arab. She was codependent in an unhappy marriage just like I was, and we would spend hours drinking and smoking cigarettes by my pool. We said our goodbyes days before I left Brazil and though we promised each other to keep in touch, the promise was one we never kept.

Sadly, I couldn't bring my two dogs who had kept me company -Amanda, our German Shepherd, and one of her puppies, Rocky. We didn't own any of the furniture in the home, so packing was fairly easy. Sadly, a family in our complex had two dogs that had been poisoned and then robbed. They had children who were devastated by the loss of their dogs. I was happy to give our dogs to this family and felt some sense of relief that they were going to a loving home. Neighbors took my other animals, which I knew they would love like I had.

BACK TO THE STATES

When we finally made it back to the States, I felt like I was returning to civilization. I could understand everyone talking around me, which was such a relief. Additionally, knowing I would still be far enough from my small town in Connecticut convinced me that things would be different. I would be different, and so would Johnny.

The first weeks in Miami, we settled in a hotel which gave us the same joy as if we were on vacation. Soon enough we found a house in Kendall, half an hour from the city of Miami, a brand new home in a residential neighborhood. I felt relieved thinking all would be new from that moment on. I would find my own pace and change my routine. I would work out and drink less. Things were looking good.

Eventually, we settled into our new home and when the excitement of the new environment wore off everything went right back to how it was in Brazil: the drinking, fighting, and isolation. Alcoholism, abuse, codependency, and narcissism do not know country boundaries. To my surprise, our nightly routine of drinking, smoking, verbal abuse and fighting followed us from Brazil. My codependency, desire to please him, and his abusive emotional words continued with a vengeance.

I had crossed that line where I knew *when* I had picked up a drink but could not tell where that first drink would lead. I was in such denial over my alcoholism that I was surprised to see that in this new place my drinking had worsened. I would drink myself unconscious, perhaps to cope with the unhappiness of emotional neglect and constant fear and abuse.

Most addicts have underlying emotional pain stored deep within from our childhood. I also found this to be true through my interactions in sessions with hundreds of patients while I worked as a therapist.

Many of us addicts grow up in dysfunctional homes where alcoholism, domestic violence, or emotional neglect had been the norm. In my case it was the latter. As a result, in adulthood we tend to gravitate toward Narcissistic partners, abusive, neglectful, or chaotic relationships and situations, even when we wish to live our life in peace. Emotional turmoil was the norm during our formative years and is what our subconscious recognizes as the "comfort zone."

The particular substance is not the issue as it is the ingrained pain that causes us to self-destruct in order to cope. Many of us are still that scared child, and it takes conscious work and effort to heal and let go in order to grow out of our self-destructive patterns.

One night in our new home, the phone rang and I picked up, happy to hear the voice on the other end—it was one of the girls from the expat community in Brazil. After a casual greeting she asked to speak with Johnny. I was stunned to find that she and my husband had been having an affair and she had told him she was five months' pregnant. We had a blowout fight that night. I had the perfect excuse to grab my bottles of Pinot Grigio and Vodka. I deserved them, because I was in pain, and had the best excuse in the world to hide myself behind a blackout and I passed out in the living room. I can't remember why it is that we never mentioned that phone call again, probably I didn't dare ask. As we became experts at doing, somehow that conversation was never touched again, nor did we hear from her again. To this day I have no idea if she was really pregnant or kept the child. Somehow, we carried on in the sick hell-marriage I had committed to.

Shortly after that episode I decided to pull myself together and find a job, which I did, as an administrative assistant at a bank. Waking up with a hangover had become another new normal for me. Some days I couldn't make it to work and other days I wasn't fit to work. It was only a matter of time before they decided to let me go.

Shortly after I got fired for showing up hungover and falling asleep on my desk, Johnny started to be late or absent from work at least one day a week, and so it came as no surprise when he was also let go.

We had worked hard on losing our jobs and were facing the consequences.

LOSING GROUND AND SOBERING UP

I was devastated with our reality and depression set in quickly. Drinking became our escape and a tool to deal with stress or to celebrate a trivial moment that made us smile. The toxic habit of drinking into late hours only clouded both of our minds, leading us to a careless and lethargic lifestyle. Sadly, we were not functioning or able to continue to pay our mortgage. I didn't care about paying my bills or credit cards, and did not even participate in the sale of the house. Johnny made all the arrangements and before I got a chance to think of my pounding head, I saw myself packing our things in the trunk of our car. He left the key inside the mailbox and that's all I can remember from that day. It was like I had been drugged.

I didn't tell my family what was happening because I was mortified and ashamed of my situation. They had all warned me and I didn't listen. I looked for freedom in all the wrong places. I know now that our constant fighting and my alcohol-fogged mind didn't let me think clearly of any other options but to stay put, which I did. I was at the mercy of his decisions and I feared him. All my dreams of being happy and rescued by marriage were an illusion. Not truly knowing myself or the woman I really was had shattered my self-esteem, and I believed I couldn't survive adulthood alone. Johnny was my only option, or so I thought.

Johnny had bought a tent and we headed to North Florida. We had no specific destination and I was too afraid to sober up and face our new reality. It was so much easier to think my life and marriage was fine, when we were not fighting, rather than face reality. It would have taken too much courage to see things for what they were, and I had none. Deep inside I knew that if I looked at the reality I would have to do something about it to make a change and most likely walk away. Instead of sobering up and thinking clearly, I continued to lose myself in my addiction.

We drove around for days until we finally arrived at Johnny's idea of a perfect vacation spot. He parked the car and got out. I glanced out the window and read a sign, "Nudist Camp, Kissimmee, Florida." I was concerned for our safety. Johnny told me to shut up and loosen up. We set up our campsite and proceeded to get to know the place. We drank with strangers and walked around naked just like everyone else there—although I usually wore a long shirt—but since I was in a constant altered state of mind, I didn't fully take in the insanity of that lifestyle. Growing up in a conservative Catholic home, sex, nudity, and living in a commune was as far from any normal I had been raised with. Many of the people in the community were very nice and friendly but they were also mostly much older than me and their life choices as couples or individuals seemed so foreign to me.

I was in my mid-twenties, jobless, constantly drunk in a loveless, abusive marriage. The only times I could sense sobriety was when I was hungover and too scared to glance back and own all the poor choices that had led me to that situation. Johnny made sure I severed ties with friends and family, which is common in narcissistic abusive relationships.

One morning I had the miraculous determination to speak up and put an end to it. "I can't take this anymore," I told Johnny. Shortly after, we packed our things, left the tent behind, and drove off.

We headed to Miami and stayed at a motel until Johnny found a job working nights at an aviation company. I felt some relief when he cashed his first paycheck; we used the money to move to a one bedroom apartment in Miami Lakes. The place was humble and small, but anything was better than a tent in the nudist camp or a cheap motel. I was delighted with his schedule because it allowed me to enjoy some peace during the evening. By then I couldn't stand the sight of him… he made my skin crawl.

One day, we were on our way to get lunch and Johnny said he needed some cash. We drove up to a bank and in the parking lot he turned to me and told me to go in and get some money. I got out of the car and walked into the bank. Back in those days there were no ATMs and you would have to fill out a slip with a bank clerk to withdraw money. I approached the counter, but when I began to fill out the slip my hand was shaking too much. The clerk filled it out for me, and I barely managed to sign my name. I was embarrassed and sweating profusely, and I told the clerk I had low blood sugar. She forced a smile and told me to hang on a minute. She came back with the bank manager and he stared at me with a poker face. He said that my signature didn't match and I explained that I had blood sugar problems and Multiple Sclerosis. He apologized and handed me the cash. To this day I have no idea how I came up with that story, but I did what I was asked to and I came out the bank with the money. When I got to the car and explained what had happened, I told Johnny I was concerned about my health. He pretended to listen, then changed the subject. Looking back, I likely had some kind of alcohol poisoning.

Tim had visited me back when Johnny and I still had a functional life in our new home in Miami. He had always disliked Johnny but after seeing his abusive manners and drinking he hated him even more. At one point during his visit he hid in the guest room during one of Johnny's tirades.

So, after being stable in one place, in our small apartment, I found the courage to call him up. I began crying and shared with him some of what I had lived to tell in the past year. I felt relieved: at last I was acknowledging to someone other than myself that what I was living in my marriage was not okay. He was horrified and very concerned. He gave me a brotherly pep talk and suggested I see a therapist. This was too deep for a brother to fix.

I took Tim's advice and searched in the Yellow Pages. I found Dr. Young and something in me pushed me to call her number in particular. From the very first session, I felt at ease and safe in her space. I felt no shame sharing my life story with her.

Dr. Young helped me see that I had no self-esteem. She became a solid mentor without judgment, especially when I told her about the outrageous anecdotes I had collected at the nudist camp and the things I experienced in Brazil with Johnny. As the days went by, I began to change, because I wanted to change. I had not been the best version of myself, not by a long shot, and I wanted to get to know the real me.

It was through one of those sessions that I realized how much resentment I harbored toward my mother. I learned what codependency meant, kind of like a person who is broken, but who tries to act as if everything's well.

Dr. Young and I spoke about my drinking habits and she expressed her suspicion that I might just be addicted to alcohol. I refused to accept that and decided to schedule my drinking episodes. "I'll only drink on weekends," I would say. When that arrangement was broken, I said "I'll drink in the evenings, but only wine." After a few weeks of lame attempts to cut back on my drinking, I realized that once I started drinking, I couldn't stop. It wasn't how many drinks or when… it was the first one that was the problem.

I trusted Dr. Young and wanted to learn about who I was. Could I live a sober life? Throughout my adulthood, alcohol had played such a major role that I had no idea what being myself without that crutch would be like.

When the day came that I found the courage to attempt my first twelve-step meeting, I sat in the parking lot simultaneously petrified and ashamed. The meeting place was called "The Friendship Club" and it was near where I lived in Miami Lakes.

The meetings were interesting to me, and I learned about the disease of alcoholism. At last I was in a place filled with people who understood my struggles. I wished I had sought out help much sooner.

At this meeting they suggested following three basics at the beginning. They're called the ABCs: A. Don't drink. B. Get a sponsor. C. Go to 90 meetings in 90 days to start. A sponsor's role is to guide you through the twelve-steps and share their experiences, strength, and hope with you. Arma was one of the ladies I often spoke with after the meetings. I was fond of her from the very first day and after my tenth meeting I asked her to become my sponsor. We quickly became close friends. She was like the sister I never had: non-judgmental, loving, and nurturing. She held my hand through my sobriety and life as I moved forward. It's been over thirty years and we're friends to this day. Over the years, she stayed sober, though I did not.

My decision to get sober motivated me to start to go jogging in the mornings and drink plenty of water. My structured way of living, clear mind, and independence infuriated Johnny on a daily basis. He didn't care to help my journey to sobriety be easier. He drank day and night, all weekend long. He hated the new sober me and my ability to not engage in arguments with him. And it was mutual: I began to dislike him to the point that the act of exchanging a single word had become a real hassle. He was an angry man before that, but as I sobered up he became more openly verbally abusive and would constantly attempt to belittle me. Looking at him with a clear mind helped me gain a new perspective on who he was, but most importantly who I was and what I was and wasn't willing to put up with anymore.

I had developed my much-needed self-respect for the first time in my adult life and I felt good about leading a healthy lifestyle.

I was determined to become independent. In my twelve-step program, they suggest no major changes in your first year of recovery, but I had no other choice. Besides my friends at the program and my therapist, I had no support system. I had to work and make enough money to move out on my own. So, after three months sober, I faxed my resume and within a week I landed a job as an administrative executive in a Fortune 500 company. Their world headquarters was located in South Miami and I was delighted. I couldn't believe that they hired me so quickly.

My self-esteem was slowly taking shape thanks to my sobriety, yet when they hired me, I couldn't help wondering what was wrong with them. Didn't they know what a train wreck I was? Couldn't they see my fear and insecurity? This new start was the beginning of living my life in consciousness and thinking clearly for the first time in my adult life.

I had asked Johnny to not drink when he came home from the graveyard shift on my first day at work. I wanted to go to my new job peacefully without any stress. He agreed but of course he didn't keep his word. He taunted me as I was getting ready for work, trying to sabotage my new start. I detested him.

I was grateful for my new job in that stunning building with all these wonderful professionals. Waking up sober and fresh every morning made me feel useful to society again, and I was proud of myself. Finally, I had a job I loved and I was very fond of my new boss. I perceived everyone as friendly and kind to one another. As I think about it today, surely my experience had to do with the fact that I was sober and could take it all in without prejudice or conspiracy theories. The nightmare I had been living seemed to be in the rearview mirror.

I did my best to ignore Johnny until we were living completely separate lives under the same roof. I worked, joined a gym, and started to socialize and go out with friends from the meetings. I worked overtime as much as I could, and stashed my earnings in a savings account. I stayed away from Johnny as much as possible.

Tim and I would speak regularly back then, sometimes several times a week. He went from being the party buddy from our college days to a loving, supporting brother. One day we were talking about my finances. My savings account was pretty slim and I'd had to buy a brand-new wardrobe and car. I didn't like to talk to Johnny, let alone ask him for money. One day, during a phone conversation with Tim I brought up the idea of divorce. To my surprise, he supported the idea and even helped me brainstorm my way out. I couldn't believe it. He suggested I go to the bank and withdraw half of our savings from our joint account, and to open an account in my own name.

I was determined to walk away, but the fear of initiating a big change was nerve-wracking. I found the courage to go to the bank one day during my lunch hour, and I did it. I opened a bank account all on my own and in my name, and it made me feel like a superhero. I was so grateful for his advice.

A few days later, Johnny found out what I had done. He felt out of control and for the first time in our marriage he attempted to raise his hand at me. He pushed me against the refrigerator and grabbed me by the neck. With a strength I didn't know I had, I pushed him away and threatened to call the police if he touched me again. I asked him to leave. That night he slept elsewhere, and when I came home from work all his things were gone. It was a miracle.

Even though he had moved out and I was moving on, I continued to feel captive. I would find myself longing for his presence sometimes, like another addiction. Even after signing the divorce papers, it took a while to cut off all ties with him.

I now know that what helped me greatly before, during, and after the divorce was that I threw myself into intensive therapy sessions. During my sessions with Dr. Young, I learned about co-dependency and addictions, what healthy love was, and the power of positive thinking. It was a time of great discovery. She was like a mother, a mentor, and a great teacher, who helped me discover a tool box of life skills and strength to draw on from these experiences.

I had been divorced for less than a year when I finally came clean with my brother and shared the truth about what had happened in my marriage, the addictions, the cheating, his affair with a woman in Brazil, my newly acquired sobriety and therapy sessions. I was grateful for his presence in my life.

I was in my late twenties when I finally accomplished full independence and got away from a toxic marriage through a divorce. Sadly, I felt like a worn-out, unattractive old woman.

Somehow, I had gotten a new job and divorced during my first year of sobriety. Although it was impossible for me to abide by the advice of no major changes during the first year, I had made my moves and I was glad I did. I was never one to follow rules anyway.

Slowly, I revived and learned to enjoy life sober with sober friends. The vast majority in my twelve-step group were young people like me. We socialized at club activities, pool parties, volleyball, and barbeques, and sometimes we'd even go out dancing as a group. After being sober for about a year, I felt I had missed out on being young and doing regular twenty-something things while I was imprisoned in my marriage. So, I started to feel restless and went out dancing and to the bars after a Friday night meeting without my group. Eventually, I slipped and came back to my recovery program again to pick up a chip to start over. In recovery we call it a "slip" when you drink during your sobriety. Groups around the world use the "chip" system to mark your road in recovery. In Florida, you picked up a white chip when you wanted to start recovery or after a "slip." After that you have three-, six-, nine-month chips until you reach your first year. Then there is a celebration with your group and family to share your experience, strength and story of hope. Anniversary nights are so powerful and special. Having family and friends at your celebration is priceless.

It amazed me from where I was that I would do that, but I did. I made up for lost time and started to date, which, as a sober person, was a new experience. Unfortunately, I still had low self-esteem, and my moral compass wasn't aligned with the concept of healthy relationships.

I dated a couple of men I had met in the rooms of recovery and quickly realized it wasn't a good idea, but at least it gave me a clear perspective on what dating sober was about, especially dating men less dysfunctional than my ex-husband. So, I focused on my sobriety and work, and cycling became my new hobby. I continued with the gym and went every morning before work.

When a great wound is healed,
There will still remain a scar.

Tao Te Ching

A NEW CHANCE AT LOVE

Sobriety was starting to feel and look good on me. I loved my job, coworkers, and boss. I was getting better at my duties every day. I was very focused, had better self-esteem, and was becoming healthy and in shape. I even quit smoking cigarettes!

Life smiled at me and I smiled right back, grateful for the opportunity to turn my life around. After a year working for the company, I felt stronger and secure of my commitment to the institution but I was beginning to get bored with my work and wanted diversity and different challenges. One afternoon, while on lunch break, I went to human resources and applied for the benefits coordinator position they had posted on the jobs board. Less than a week went by before I learned that I had gotten the job. I couldn't believe my luck.

I was thrown into that new field with barely any training. It wasn't rocket science, but the challenge did overwhelm me. I started to question myself and my abilities. I loved working with people and the change of responsibilities had awakened my ambitious spirits. I was focused and despite a lack of training by my supervisor I quickly learned as I worked. When in doubt, I would ask my superiors confidently; they were thrilled with my enthusiasm and I with their feedback. For the first time in my life, I was getting praise for a job well done. The broken girl from Connecticut was a shadow from my past. I was building my new self and became more comfortable with me each day. The days of toxic abuse in a helpless marriage were far away, and so were the memories of my addiction. I had been sober for over a year and was forgetting my past too soon.

Now I was ready to be on the dating scene, but no one sparked my interest enough for long. Most of the guys at my job were married and the single men I knew at the company were simply not an option.

One morning, while serving myself a cup of coffee in the break room, my coworker pointed at a guy we had never seen in our office before. "Hey, Lynn," she said. "Look at that guy coming down the hall. I think he's going to your office," she leaned against the door to keep it open as I walked past.

My coworker was right. That handsome guy had just walked into my office and had taken the liberty to sit down by my desk, apparently waiting for me. I quickly fixed my dress, pulling it down to flatten any creases and briskly sat at my desk in front of him. As I introduced myself I sensed butterflies in my stomach. I hadn't felt anything like that in so long. His name was Carlos and he had black hair, a mustache, and deep brown eyes with a direct gaze. *He's not from Florida*, I thought. Turns out I was right, he was from Puerto Rico.

My role in the company was to enroll employees in their benefit plan and since he was new, he had come to discuss his benefits in the company. For the first time in a long time I was curious about someone. The minute he left my office, I couldn't help but peek at the file I had just shoved in my desk, and I was happy to learn that he was single. Reading through it made me smile. My best friend at work, Grace, came in to get the scoop on the new guy and I told her he wasn't married. After preparing his file, the only potential glitch I saw was that Carlos had an eight-year-old daughter. I had never dated a man with a child and was not interested in anything to do with kids at that point in my life. I didn't know if he would like me but in case he did, at least his single status would be a good start.

Carlos started working at the company the next day and we got to know each other. I'd find any excuse to bring papers to his desk or any type of documents related to his newly acquired employment status (which could have gone in the mail). He was six years younger than me but I didn't care. I had previously picked older men and this was refreshing for me. I was taking care of myself since getting sober and I worked out daily. Not wasting money on late-night outings or smoking provided me with the spare money I spent at the salon and on great clothes and shoes.

Carlos and I spoke every day, and we went out to lunch at least twice a week. At Christmas we went together to the corporate holiday party and he was surprised to see that I liked dancing salsa. He noticed I didn't pick up a drink and I was glad to see he wasn't much of a drinker. There was a Latin band playing and we danced the night away. By the end of the night, our love story had begun.

I had enough experience to see how stimulating it was to be with a man whose life didn't revolve around alcohol. Coming from an abusive marriage, my barometer for picking men wasn't always trustworthy. As I got sober and healthier with therapy I started to believe that I was worthy of being loved the way I wanted to be loved. I was clear that I didn't want anything to do with an abusive man or one with addictions.

Carlos seemed so different. I really didn't have any indicator on relationships, so I was doing the best I could at the time. I did know that he was not abusive, did not drink (only very little socially), and we had a strong attraction to each other. He seemed to be an educated man from a good family.

By the following year we were dating exclusively and I eventually found the courage to tell him about my drinking problem and my recovery. My sponsor had a long talk with me about the subject the night before and had given me the much-needed support that helped me stand up for myself. I felt some shame as I shared my issues with him, but the fact that he didn't know much about the disease of alcoholism helped me stand strong. He embraced my honesty and hugged me before telling me how proud he was of me and my accomplishments. Nevertheless, I wasn't ready to explain in detail about the extent of my drinking problem.

I gave the illusion that I was fine being around his friends and coworkers drinking and attending and hosting many parties. In reality, I wasn't okay, and I started to long to drink "normally" like him and his friends. How could he drink a few drinks and then stop? If he could do it, surely I could, too. *It's a matter of willpower*, I said to myself.

During one of our social events I was on the way to the Ladies' Room when a uniformed waiter walked by carrying a round tray. I grabbed a glass of champagne and he barely noticed. Shortly after that the party was over and so was my sobriety. I ended the night so drunk that I blacked out and Carlos had to carry me to the car. Poor Carlos had no idea what was happening—and all that because of a short trip to the Ladies Room and a split-second decision to end my sobriety.

The next day I was mortified and I was glad I could barely remember anything. I made excuses, mainly to myself, but soon enough the shame sank in thinking he was better than me. The man I loved had witnessed that dark ugly side of me. Sadly, he still had no idea about the depth of my disease of alcoholism. I had somehow managed to convince him with a story about why I acted the way I did and felt horrible. I was confused and angry with myself.

I quickly returned to my home group to pick up a white chip at the end of the meeting. A white chip is what they hand out to those looking to get sober, or have returned from a slip as a symbolic and tangible commitment to ourselves. I had to start counting days of sobriety again. Unfortunately for me, I had carelessly awakened the beast of addiction and now I had less control than ever before.

I had heard many stories about people who had had bouts of sobriety and then went back to their old drinking lifestyles and never made it back to the meetings. Some had died from their alcoholism and others might as well have died—their lives had become nothing but a collection of misfortunes. Some became homeless, and for some lucky others, jail had saved them from themselves and they had found sobriety there. Possibly, they felt that being locked up was about the best thing that could have happened to them.

I knew I didn't want to end up as part of those statistics. I had to put my best foot forward and learn to nourish my mind and body and build the strength I knew I could regain through sobriety and attending meetings.

I slipped a number of times and was frustrated that I couldn't drink "normally," like Carlos and his friends did. God knows I tried. I had never been with a man who drank normally, and I desperately wanted to fit in. It baffles me to this day that I had apparently forgotten how far and low my drinking had taken me and how it had stripped me of my dignity, self-worth, and health. I continued going to the meetings and after a couple of months with my struggle, I was finally able to get back on track with the program. Things seemed to be okay.

It was 1992 and Carlos and I had been dating for several months. Life seemed surreal and blissful and was intense. And then life drastically changed once again. One morning as I was getting ready for work, I looked in the mirror to inspect my face—I tended to be overly critical and sensitive when it came to my face. Upon first glance, I thought I had slept wrong, as the right side of my face looked tired, or as if it had pillow marks. I tried to smooth it a bit and I still looked tired. Something wasn't right. *No! This can't be happening again!*, I cried out loud… I couldn't process what I was seeing. Sixteen years later, high school was happening all over again.

I was in total disbelief. *Why? My life was going so perfectly.* Within the hour my face had become paralyzed on the same right side. It was then I realized no amount of smoothing was going to fix it.

I immediately called my parents in Connecticut and quickly reverted to that 18-year-old schoolgirl once again. Sobbing, trying to sound coherent, I told them what was happening. They were so distraught that they were not in Florida to console me. All they could do was suggest I call Carlos and have him come over to help me. I didn't have the courage or strength to call him myself but I obediently gave them his number. I also didn't want him to see me like this, but I didn't want to be alone.

Instinctively, I started to pull all the blinds closed in the apartment, which became the darkness I once knew. My intentions were to conceal my disfigurement from Carlos, the world, and even from myself.

There it was… the knock at the door. I was terrified for him to see me. Just as I was about to tell him not to come in, I heard his gentle voice and I knew I needed to be with him. I opened the door and started sobbing against his comforting chest—I wouldn't let him look at me. He assured me all would be well, despite my terror and shame.

We called for an emergency appointment with a doctor. Scarf wrapped around my face, we left for the hospital. All the while Carlos was telling me everything would be okay, which I was not so sure of, but I hung onto those words.

Once inside the doctor's office I was looking for some kind of confirmation that this was just temporary and would pass. Unfortunately, this doctor was all business. Diagnostics and treatment options were different now than they had been when I was in high school, and the doctor immediately ordered an MRI of the brain.

The next day I went for the MRI and I returned a few days later to pick up my results. While I waited, my mind went to a dark place. I was so fearful I could barely speak. *What if I have Bell's palsy again? What if it's brain cancer? What if I look like this for the rest of my life?*

The door opened and the doctor entered with a stone-cold face. He quickly pulled out my results and projected the MRI images onto the wall. In a very monotonous voice, he stated: "Your MRI shows several small brain tumors. One of them is in your ear canal—it's called an acoustic neuroma. This tumor is pressing on your seventh nerve along the nerves to the facial muscle, causing pressure and weakness."

I was listening but not really comprehending. Mostly I was taken aback by his matter-of-fact description of what they found. No compassion or pauses. My head was spinning and my heart was pounding. I grabbed Carlos's hand right before I passed out onto the floor.

After what seemed forever, I came to and was sitting in a chair looking at the same stony-faced doctor, who proceeded to tell me my options. The good news was all tumors were benign. They would monitor the growth of the acoustic neuroma and brain tumors with annual MRIs. He couldn't tell me if I had actually had Bell's palsy in high school or if all along it had been the tumor pressing on the nerve in my ear canal that caused the facial weakness.

He also suggested I immediately start physical therapy with nerve stimulation and facial massages. He also gave me steroids to stop the weakness and strengthen the muscles. With that, we left and went on our way.

Eventually the treatments worked and my face returned to about 98% of normal strength and appearance. The weakness on the right side of my face was noticeable when I was tired. I focused on running, working out, and taking care of my husband and career with a vengeance.

Around this time I also made the decision to register and return to college to finish my Bachelor's Degree. Carlos was always supportive, and after a year of dating we got married. This time it was the kind of wedding I wanted.

We planned everything carefully and saved enough money to pay for a beautiful reception. It was my dream wedding. Just like I had always wanted, we got married by the ocean with a minister from the Unity Church. The ceremony as well as the party took place in a beautiful hotel, the Sonesta Beach Resort, overlooking the ocean in Key Biscayne, Florida. This time everybody approved of my new husband and I walked down the aisle with great pride, hope, and happiness. I adored his family and life seemed surreal. I got married as a sober woman and I felt very proud of my tenacity and courage. What a beautiful life I was living. It seemed like a fairytale come true.

My greatest fear was that I would have children and do to them what had been done to me. I wouldn't let that happen. Dating a man that had a child was something new and a bit intimidating for me. When we started dating, Carlos had told me about his daughter, Missy, from his first marriage, who was nine years old when we met. She was living in Puerto Rico with her mother at that time. So, I felt relieved that I did not have to deal with a child or share him with anybody else. Yes, I was selfish with my newfound love! Later that year, his daughter and ex-wife decided to move to Florida so she could be closer to her dad. Initially, I wasn't thrilled about doing any kind of coparenting. Life seemed to change for us after Missy's arrival. Yet after some growing pains for all of us, Missy and I became good friends—to this day I keep in touch with her and love her very much. She taught me that I just might be a good mother some day, as I eventually got into a parenting mode when she stayed with us, which surprised me.

Since we started dating, Carlos had stated his desire for more children in response to which I would often go quiet. Somehow, with time and a loving marriage, I warmed up to the idea and a year later I became pregnant with my daughter. I had been working on myself, facing my childhood issues and fears with my therapist for over a year before Carlos and I met. This work had helped me come to terms with the idea that I would be a good, kind, loving mom. I vowed I would never hit my children or punish them as I was… And I never did!

Sobriety was easy, as there was no way I was going to drink during my pregnancy. While pregnant I entered an advanced Master's Program at Florida International University. I was older than most of the students in the program and felt a bit out of place. Returning to the classroom as a sober woman was an interesting experience. My new life and a clear head, thanks to my sobriety, proved that I wasn't the lazy and forgetful student I once was. This time I was an extremely responsible 'A' student with impeccable attendance. I'm proud to say that I graduated with Honors, which surprised and inspired even me.

I went to class up until the very last week of my pregnancy. That day, I had gotten out of bed feeling a bit drowsy and unusually bloated, but paid no mind and went to my morning class anyway. In the middle of class I felt the urge to go to the bathroom and I walked out unaware of the trail of blood so heavy that it seeped through my pants and dripped to the very ground as I walked out. The girls in class looked on in horror and followed me out.

"What's your doctor's number?!" one of them yelled out and as I turned my head, I almost fainted.

There was blood all over the floor and the bottom half of my clothes were drenched. One of the students rushed me to the hospital. Upon arrival at the emergency room the nurses buzzed around me with monitors and whispering about the situation. I was very anxious and wished my husband were there.

The doctor quickly arrived and told me that the baby's umbilical cord was wrapped around her neck and detaching from the placenta. The baby would need to be delivered via an emergency Cesarean section. I watched a nurse pick up a phone to call my husband. I wasn't allowed to move, and didn't have a chance to speak with him. I was terrified.

Carlos left his office in Fort Lauderdale and raced down to South Miami Hospital, arriving within half an hour, and we could at least see each other for a short moment before they rushed me into surgery. All went well during the operation and our first child was born completely healthy and I thanked God for that. We named her Jessica Lynn. The first thing I wanted to know was if she had all her fingers and toes. Smiling, Carlos said, "Yes, and she's beautiful."

After the C-section I was pumped up with Morphine for the pain, which I found quite comforting. I never thought to tell the doctors that I was a recovering alcoholic. The first rule of thumb for sobriety is honesty. Hiding this information seemed to open that door of addiction once more. But because I was under prescribed medication, I told myself that all was well. After I was discharged, the doctor gave me Percocet to deal with the continued pain from the incision. Again I conveniently failed to alert the doctor that I was in alcohol recovery. By hiding my past, I jeopardized my sobriety once again. The pills became "Mommy's little helper," which I longed for frequently during my recuperation.

THE BABY

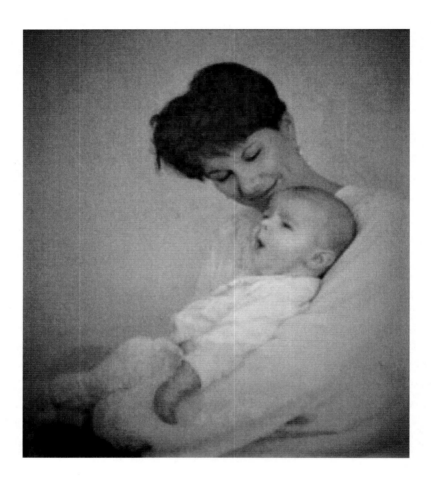

Given my upbringing and my past, I was hesitant about my ability to be a mother. I feared not being fit to parent and I wasn't confident that I would be a good mother. My parents came from Connecticut to help us with the baby, which I was grateful for. The C-section was more painful than I was up for and the confinement to a bed at home was overwhelming. Just to cough or roll over was a daunting task, and painful. I was used to running daily and going to the gym to lift weights. I was not one to lie in bed for long. I had been a single woman taking care of my own needs for so long. So this new lifestyle and a little human being constantly depending on me was more than I felt ready to handle.

After about two weeks on the Percocet, I asked for a refill for the "continued pain." Actually, I just liked the high. Dad was blunt—he stared at me, his face drawn and troubled, and said, "I don't think you need to keep taking those drugs, do you?" I agreed, feeling like a child whose candy had been snatched out of her hands. I stopped taking the pills, but only after I finished the whole bottle a few days later. Nevertheless, I longed for the buzz: the mood-altering sensations from the painkillers left me aching for more.

My life seemed to suddenly unravel with chaos and became overwhelming. The course load of this intense one-year Master's program along with new motherhood became too much for me to bear. I had been sober for a little over a year, but my old insecurities started to kick in. *How do other mothers do this?* Nursing and pumping for my baby before going to school became too much pressure for me. After a few weeks, I noticed I couldn't produce enough milk to feed my baby. That morning I burst out crying in desperation. I felt like such a failure.

My mother-in-law, visiting from Puerto Rico, came into my room when she heard my cries. After listening to my frustrations, she hugged me gently and offered much-needed words of support. She explained that for some women breastfeeding is simply not an option and she assured me that my child would be just fine.

Shortly afterwards we made an appointment with the pediatrician and thankfully he approved of putting Jessica on formula. I was relieved and instantly felt less guilty. I wanted to be the best mother I could be, but not at the cost of all that anxiety.

I was happy to stop nursing and looked forward to getting back in my groove. I was sad, irritable, and restless all the time. I wanted to run again, which always made me feel wonderful. I thought, once I can start to work out, I'll feel better.

One evening around that time, on one of those typical family dinner nights with my parents and spouse, I asked my husband for a glass of wine. He didn't say anything about it and served me as if my drinking problem was nonexistent. But my parents gave me a look right away. I didn't care. I held them responsible for my slip, since they drank heavily in front of me daily. I felt a unique sense of relief the moment I took that first sip. There was a special touch of bliss coating my lips and the back of my throat, instantly giving me a warm sense of comfort and joy. Nobody was going to take that feeling away from me.

That one glass of wine had opened the door, leading me into the delusion that if I drank wine that one night and had managed my drinking, perhaps I wasn't an alcoholic after all. Perhaps my problem was about my impulsive nature and poor coping skills. That mentality drove me to slip here and there for brief periods, compromising my sobriety. The lapses between drinking episodes became shorter with time until I found myself drinking wine almost every night.

Life continued as a mother, student, and wife. After struggling more than I liked to admit with my drinking back then, I finally returned to recovery and the program and I promised myself this time I wouldn't let anything or anyone screw it up. I was very proud to bring my baby with me to meetings and to announce that she would never have to see me drunk. I was grateful.

Shortly after picking up that sobriety chip, we had houseguests. They drank moderately and they loved their pot. One night they were outside smoking pot. I popped my head out to ask them if they needed anything. Only I knew that my concerns for their needs at that time was not the real reason.

"You guys okay out here?" I asked.

"Yes, we're good… Want a hit?" Just like that I was back in the game and off the wagon. The next day I drank some wine and started to sneak drinks periodically from then on after that. The beast was out of the cage. Eventually I realized that the emotional and physical pain I was in by trying to face my addiction alone had become unbearable. I decided to return to the wonderful therapist I had found a while back during my divorce and first attempt at sobriety.

Dr. Young was almost as happy to see me as I was to see her. She was a big part of my life and she helped me turn my life around. Thanks to her, I eventually left the corporate high-paying job where I had met Carlos. Never would I have imagined that I would be back in school and change careers so dramatically. Grateful for her guidance and expertise, I felt the calling to go back to school to become a therapist. I wanted to touch people's lives like she had touched mine.

After a few sessions where I complained about the people and program she made several suggestions: "Go to another room if you don't like those people." "Or go to a professional group in a different part of town." I had excuses for everything, trying to convince her that her suggestions were not such a great idea. She became exhausted with my resistance.

Finally, one day she said very matter-of-factly, "Lynn, you need to pick a side." I was confused.

"What? It's not that simple!" I complained.

"Pick a side!" she insisted. "Are you in or out of the program?"

Stubborn rebel that I was, I chose to stay out of the program, and I told her, "I don't need those people, really! I got this." I believed that to be true more times than I can count.

Carlos and I drank together when it seemed convenient for him and the nights he chose to go dry I felt shame because of my desire to drink without him. I felt like a child who was constantly getting into trouble and I became resentful and bitter about everything and everyone else.

Along with having an active addiction came shame. I was frustrated trying to balance different roles in my life while trying to keep my drinking a secret. I liked to curse a lot and he scolded me for it and even criticized my housekeeping skills. I thought I was immaculate at cleaning. I couldn't take that sort of criticism, I had to be perfect. I worried about my looks and my skills in the kitchen; I considered myself a good cook but that, too, wasn't enough.

Sometimes I did manage to surprise him with romantic ideas and his approval lifted my spirits. I didn't realize then that my identity was intertwined with his opinion of me. As time went on I was turning into that insecure person I once was. In his defense, he never knew what truck was about to hit him with my drinking and I didn't know it either. All I knew was that I wanted to drink like a normal person and felt constant shame from my inability to do so.

I eventually graduated from Florida International University with high honors in Family Counseling. The night before my graduation my parents came from Connecticut to celebrate the occasion and we spent the night eating and drinking. I drank one way in front of them and then privately sneaked drinks out of sight. The next day I could only count the minutes to go back to bed. I had to endure my own graduation ceremony with a severe hangover.

After graduation, I got a part-time job in a clinic working with the elderly. It was the start of my career, a way to get experience and a part-time job. This position as a counselor allowed me to work and take care of my daughter while earning enough to help out with the bills. Shortly after, we purchased a new four-bedroom home. The house was located in a family-oriented neighborhood on a beautiful lake in Plantation, Florida. It had a built-in screened pool, fruit trees, and even wild ducks. It all seemed so perfect.

And yet I had no close family nearby, and loneliness triggered my anxiety. I blamed Carlos for leaving me alone so much while working all the time. I found solace and support in my drinking in the evenings. I was like a vampire: when the sun went down, baby in bed, house cleaned, out came the bottle and a cigarette. I never drank during the day and absolutely hated the smell of cigarettes. But give me a drink, and out they came. This became routine since Carlos travelled so much.

Since I was able to care for my child, work, clean the house, cook daily, and go to the gym, I had the illusion that I was okay. Recovery seemed so far away. I stopped calling my best friend and sponsor at the time. Though this was devastating for me, deceiving her had become painful and exhausting, so I stopped all communication. She had no idea that I was drinking again, as I had moved almost an hour away from her and the club rooms. Anybody that I was close to in the program was gone or far away. I did have one "normal" friend from work that I loved. She was married, too, and had her own life with a new baby. Being distant from her took its toll on our friendship, and my schedule before the baby left little time to meet new friends. I became very skilled at hiding my reality from everybody.

I was consumed with housework and often overwhelmed by parenting, but I knew that it was all worth it. I loved my daughter. Jessica always managed to put a smile on my face regardless of how hard my day had been. It seemed that I constantly needed to entertain or give of myself to make any kind of peace at home with Carlos and this constant pull from my independence was daunting. To make matters worse, he traveled frequently and I had no family of my own in the area. Jessica and I were completely alone most of the time.

In an attempt to find myself again I went back into my old exercise routine and started to run and work out at the gym. Exercise gave me a sense of accomplishment. Looking back at those days, I wonder if I had postpartum depression. Those first few months of motherhood were dark days for me. As happy as I was while mothering a beautiful healthy baby, I couldn't understand why I was down most of the time and felt helpless with a constant fear for the wellbeing and life of my baby.

MOVING TO PUERTO RICO

Carlos came home from work one day and informed me his company was shutting down their regional office in Fort Lauderdale. He still had a job if he wanted… but in Puerto Rico. We had six weeks to move or he was out of a job. I went into panic mode. *Move again?! We just purchased our new home! Puerto Rico?* Carlos was delighted, as he was from there and had family. So, the move was exciting for him. I, on the other hand, had many concerns.

"You have the final word," he told me. "It's up to you if we go or not."

Great, I thought, *and ruin his career?*

Life continued to present me with surprises and decisions to be made. Another turn indeed… to an island? I loved our new four-bedroom home on a beautiful lake, as well as decorating every corner of it. Move out of my cookie-cutter neighborhood with my people, language, and culture? I had previously visited Puerto Rico with Carlos on vacation on a couple of occasions. Those trips gave me the opportunity to actually see what life was like on the island. Twenty years ago, the conditions were much different than they are now. *No*, I thought. *I didn't want to go. I won't go!*

The decision to move to Puerto Rico brought back flashbacks of Brazil and I began to feel traumatized all over again. I had to remind myself that I wasn't that confused, naïve 23-year-old anymore, with an abusive husband.

Shortly after our discussion, I found out I was pregnant with our second child. I had previously lost two pregnancies, so this news further added to my level of anxiety about moving. After Jessica was born, I was open to trying for a second child. The first loss after her birth came as a surprise when we were at the doctor's visit to look at the sonogram for the first time. As the doctor was doing the exam, she said "I am so sorry… there is no heartbeat." The baby was only about six weeks along. Initially, we were shocked and very sad. But after a brief period of grieving, I was able to come to a place of acceptance. Shortly after that loss I became pregnant again. This time I tried to believe all would be well and took extra care of my already-rigid workout and health routine, although at this point I was binge-drinking on weekends. My second miscarriage happened further along and was more devastating. We were asleep at home one morning when I started to have excruciating pain and went to the bathroom. I was miscarrying in the toilet with blood clots and did not even realize it. After a time, my husband came in and said he was going to take me to the emergency room. Upon examination and giving me pain medicine for the severe cramps, the doctor informed us that I had lost the baby and they were going to perform a dilation and curettage procedure. We were devastated and went through our grieving process more profoundly this time. The idea of becoming pregnant again meant apprehension of another loss. Somehow this made us a stronger couple and we supported each other through the process, once again.

I feared leaving the States and my doctors on the mainland during the pregnancy. But I didn't have a full-time job and Carlos's company had excellent benefits and opportunities for him. So, I felt

I had no choice but to support my husband, and I eventually said yes and the whirlwind began.

We had to quickly sell our new home and go on another house-hunting trip, but this time in Puerto Rico. We flew to Puerto Rico with two-year-old Jessica and my morning sickness to start looking for a home again. A realtor was arranged for us through the company to see several houses the day after we arrived. As we got into his car I started to have second thoughts about the decision. I whispered to Carlos, "This is the car he is taking us out in?" It was old and not very nice with weak air-conditioning. Carlos was always good at smoothing my ruffled feathers and assured me it would be alright. I was pregnant, cranky, and scared.

After seeing a few houses with bars on the windows, garbage, and chickens on the streets, I started to feel nauseous. I wasn't used to seeing animals in the streets and abandoned cars and I wasn't sure if it was my early pregnancy kicking in or my dismay at what I was experiencing. What was happening to my life? I felt like I was taking a step backwards in our lifestyle and immediately regretted my decision to come. I already missed our new home on the lake.

Eventually, we realized that living in a secure gated community was the best way for us in terms of safety and comfort, and after much complaining from me, Carlos found us a beautiful home with a guarded entrance and full amenities. The neighborhood was a great place to jog and raise a family. I was somewhat on board now, though still skeptical.

Carlos had gone to Puerto Rico ahead of us to get oriented on the job, while I tied things up with the house packing and went to doctors' visits. When the actual moving day came, I was so grateful to be carrying a healthy baby and getting to approximately six months with no problems. This was such a relief for me and Carlos. Upon arrival in San Juan we were initially put up in a hotel in Isla Verde. So, at first this experience felt like a vacation and I was able to walk to the beach and hear English all day. *Maybe this won't be so bad?* Expenses were being paid by the company while we were in the hotel and our new home was being prepared for our move in.

I spent the days with my daughter on the beach while my husband worked. If we were hungry, the hotel had anything we needed. I even was excited to meet other Americans who were on vacation there.

Finally, our home was ready, and once we left the hotel bubble, my real challenges began to surface and reality sunk in. I had no knowledge of Spanish and I struggled daily with the language and lack of any friends. I was lonely again, and I felt isolated. I missed my culture and neighborhood. I even missed the job I had disliked so much, as it was something that was mine and that I was good at.

I tried to get to know the neighbors, who were very friendly, but my inability to speak Spanish was a huge obstacle in getting to know people. I had only taken Spanish in high school and one class in college. I took up Spanish lessons and tried to immerse myself in the culture. My Puerto Rican neighbors were very kind and patient with me. But I believe they embraced my efforts and I was pleasantly surprised by their warmth and acceptance.

We found out that I was having a boy and I was very excited and anxious to bring him into the world. My concern about the medical care was ever-present, especially given the lack of English-speaking nurses in the hospital.

In the midst of the move and getting accustomed to our new home and at eight months pregnant, life threw another curve ball. Hurricane George was approaching the island. We weren't really prepared for George other than hurricane shutters. We didn't have a generator and I was dreading what I heard was about to hit us. I had lived through Hurricane Andrew in Miami when I first met Carlos, and that was bad enough. George was supposed to be worse and we had a toddler and I was very pregnant.

Somehow, we survived that huge hurricane. The wind was so intense that I started having contractions. Carlos had been injured while putting up the shutters and had one arm in a sling. Thankfully, he didn't have to try to deliver our baby with only one arm.

BABY PETER ARRIVES

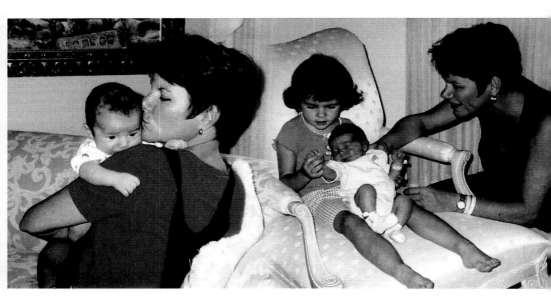

After the hurricane passed, the island was almost in complete shut-down mode, and food, ice, and water were scarce. My parents had already purchased plane tickets to come for Peter's birth. Once they arrived, they were struggling with the hurricane's aftermath along with us.

The day came that my son was ready to come into the world, in Puerto Rico! We went to the hospital without any emergency or complications this time. The entire experience of giving birth in an-other culture was a bit daunting. I was hesitant to be left alone, as I did not speak Spanish fluently at all. Carlos and his mom were at my side constantly, which was a great comfort. My mom and dad were taking care of Jessica at home.

We then headed home with our son. Life on the island with two babies was a lot for me. Just going to the grocery store or a pharmacy to find things with a toddler and newborn kept me from venturing out, but I also didn't do well confined to the house. I missed jogging and going to the gym. So, I was forced to be creative to exercise at home. Eventually Carlos bought me a baby jogger and I could jog with Peter when my daughter was in daycare.

I soon regained my rhythm of weekend drinking and the socializing and parties continued. I was drawn to the drinking and amount of socializing that was on the island. Gradually, it all took a toll on our marriage. We went to counseling to try to get some relief, which it maybe did for a while. The psychologist was always telling me privately that he could "help" me regarding my drinking. But I was in no way ready to go cold turkey and I didn't know how I'd cope with everything I was feeling and my frustrations without self-medicating in the evenings.

All along, I was always a good mother and attended to my home, meals, and children, and I always took care of my spouse, too. I was always striving to be perfect and my perception at the time was that I came up short.

I always made efforts to make birthdays and holidays special for my kids. Thankfully, today they say that's one of their fondest memories. Jessica always lightens my heart when she tells me of all the good memories she has of me as a mother. I had my flaws for sure, but I did my best under the circumstances.

To live with shame daily due to addiction is a horrible thing to endure. Many people don't understand this. I would wake up with a hangover and think, *If only I didn't drink and smoke, I would be okay, a good woman.* What an illusion! Sneaking and hiding the true beast I had within was exhausting. I would long for the sun to set and the children to go to bed so I could be with my lovers: Pinot Grigio and Marlboro Lights. The first cigarette was always disgusting and forced until I was on my second glass of wine. *Ahh... There we go!*

I loved my family, but I was always feeling broken and not enough.

Somewhere along the line I lost my balance about where I was and how to be happy. Constant criticism tore at me and I longed for it to end or not be affected by it. I just wanted someone to see me—not my body, clothes, or how I cleaned, cooked, or spoke. That never seemed to happen. I had a lonely tormented soul that even I could not fix.

LIFE WITH TWO BABIES

All my discomfort and challenges moving to Puerto Rico with a toddler and going through the hurricane shook me to my core. I had no support system to lean on and I felt like a fish out of water in my new environment. Carlos continued working a lot. Sadly, he really couldn't understand my struggle. Not having close friends or family to talk with on the island furthered my unhappiness.

The island had few signs to mark roads or highways before the hurricane, now there were none. A simple trip to a store was more than I could handle with a toddler and being pregnant. I got lost all the time. My struggle with island life and the aftermath of the hurricane became a heaviness that weighed on me every day, as did the pregnancy. Eventually, delivery day came and I was intent on having a natural birth, which the doctors were able to concede. The nurses at the hospital didn't speak English and I had a rough time trying to communicate what I needed when Carlos was not there. Somehow, I managed.

I'd had no idea of the vast differences in care compared to my first delivery on the mainland. You had to bring your own everything... blankets, extra pillow, toiletries, sanitary pads for after the birth, and you even had to buy the pitcher for water and bedpan in the pharmacy. I complained daily to Carlos, and he assured me all would be fine. He didn't feel the same discomforts that I was experiencing at all. He was so content to be back on his island and with his family and a job he was enjoying. Although I had agreed to relocate, my resentments and hormones from the birth of my son were beginning to haunt me.

Now I had two little ones depending on me! Shortly after returning home from the hospital, the evening meals with my parents and Carlos and their drinking in front of me started up again. I longed for a glass of wine and held off for as long as I could.

After approximately eleven months sober, one night at the table with everybody drinking, I poured a glass of wine and took a long-awaited sip. With that familiar soothing feeling came the looks and comments from those at the table, including from Carlos. At that point, I simply didn't care and continued to have my drink. After all, I deserved it! Look what I had just been through.

I was determined to allow myself a drink from time to time, which at first was manageable but quickly became more frequent, and then necessary. I continued to struggle with my lack of friends, language barrier, and two babies to care for.

I loved when my parents would visit. We would travel all over Puerto Rico with the kids and rent beach houses and enjoy the island as much as we could with them. When they were gone, I missed having a close family unit. As I had no family of my own on the island, my extended Puerto Rican family became my inner circle. Thankfully, I liked my in-laws and would have them over frequently. They loved my cooking and I loved entertaining and having my drinks while they visited.

I longed for some kind of professional outlet to use my skills as a therapist again. My brother-in-law was a friend of a top psychologist on the island who had a well-known mental health clinic, as well as published articles in the newspaper. I soon learned that who you know on the island was very important for building relationships. He was able to get me an interview with his contact when I was nine months pregnant. She was impressed with me and wanted a gringa on the team to work with her English-speaking clients in the clinic. She said that the job was mine when I was ready. I couldn't believe my luck and the opportunity that awaited me.

So, after healing and taking care of my babies for six months, I was feeling anxious to be a working person again. I started to work part time at the clinic. It gave me the opportunity to work, to be of service, and to still take care of my children. I felt I had the best of both worlds. I finally felt my old self coming back, a ray of hope. Getting dressed in a suit and attending patients lifted my spirits and the depression I had been feeling.

At the beginning of our relocation and not working full time, I managed to leave the island frequently to visit Connecticut with the children. Now that they were older and in school and preschool, and I was working, our trips became less frequent. I missed connecting with my family and I wanted my children to know their American culture and get to know their grandparents, aunts, uncles, and cousins.

Life became a whirlwind of parties with Carlos's colleagues and celebrations, which seemed to never end. This kind of lifestyle, which I initially embraced, was very dangerous for my addiction and things started to progressively get worse. I often dreaded the idea of gatherings, which I found extremely loud, as well as hurt my one functioning ear. I often wanted to leave, to go have a drink and some quiet. I knew that I couldn't, and I know that Carlos only became annoyed when he sensed my irritability. At one point Carlos asked me why I didn't just alternate drinks with water. Now, that's a lovely idea to someone who doesn't understand addiction. I would have loved to have been savvy enough to pull that off. But once I started to enjoy the drink and the party, water was not an option for me. I loved the buzz and the escape.

I was usually social, but once I started to drink I became more outgoing, funny and wild... I loved to dance. And then I would search for a cigarette. This behavior really disturbed Carlos, and I assume it embarrassed him as well. I absolutely adored fashion and dressing up. Once I knew we had a gala or festivity to go to, my heart would quicken and I would plan months ahead on everything from hair, makeup, shoes, the perfect dress, and how to look as fabulous as I could, though I never felt fabulous enough. I became obsessed with trying to run the house well, take care of the kids, and be the perfect wife. After both births I had quickly gotten my figure back and was always conscious of my weight and body. I was a dedicated gym rat and was running or at a spinning class or doing weights daily. My kitchen pantry looked like Vitamin World with all my pills and shakes, anti-aging and health-food stash.

Back at the clinic, my secretary didn't speak English and communication was often a challenge. The business etiquette and ethics I had been taught in the fast-paced corporate world did *not* work in my new culture. Though I strove to fit in as well as continue to learn the language as much as I could, I often found myself unintentionally offending people with my style. When we arrived in Puerto Rico Carlos's company paid for Spanish lessons and I was able to learn some basic things before Peter's birth.

My children would soon become bilingual being exposed to Spanish as young children, and I agreed to enroll them in Spanish-speaking daycare and schools, which many expats didn't do. In an effort to support families relocating to Puerto Rico and the high cost of living, most companies usually offered expats a package for support during the entire process, including educational costs, language classes, housing, and car expenses. Unfortunately, we were not considered expats—we were just lucky to have a job, though we did receive some relocation and housing assistance.

Carlos and I had married in 1993, a year and a half after the Bell's palsy incident. Fast forward seven years and my annual MRI showed that the tumors in my ear had grown slightly. By then we were no longer in Florida and the surgeons in Puerto Rico recommended brain surgery to remove the tumor, which meant the possibility of permanent facial paralysis and other complications. We did intensive research on other, less invasive treatments for Acoustic Neuroma in the States. Eventually, I opted for a consultation in Maryland at John Hopkins Hospital. They offered a procedure called fractionated radioactive surgery (FSR), which would require small radiation treatments to the tumor over a period of two weeks, no surgery involved. This sounded much safer and more reasonable, and eventually I went back for the treatment. While we were there we also took advantage of seeing Carlos's daughter, Missy, who had moved to Maryland with her mother.

The treatment process was horrific for me as I suffer from claustrophobia. The FSR involved wearing a fitted mask and going into a tunnel machine for about an hour every other day for two weeks. I requested heavy anxiety medication for before, during, and after the experience in the machine. I had been doing "controlled" drinking fairly well, but during that time my drinking increased, along with my anxiety, fear, and smoking, which I normally detested.

Once the treatment was done and the tumor in the ear canal was killed successfully, I was again advised to continue with yearly MRIs to monitor the other benign tumors. To date, everything has remained unchanged. Once I entered the world of healing and holistic approaches for myself and my clients, my intentions regarding the tumors changed. I received extensive energy healing from several healers over the past years in recovery, and I have also provided healings and meditations for myself.

I have come to see my tumors as light energy and a positive thing, which I no longer fear. I continue to have facial weakness which I am aware of daily and try to conceal to the extent possible. It is interesting for me that even with this issue affecting my self-image, along my spiritual journey I now have a career where people look at me for a living, either as a therapist or a guest speaker.

The decision to enroll my children in all Spanish-speaking daycare and schools was great for them and frustrating for me. I often had challenges understanding family meetings or trying to speak with teachers at the school, which often kept me oblivious to topics most of the time and frustrated. Many teachers didn't know or want to speak English, and my language handicap left me reluctant to participate or be present at activities or school programs. I most likely would have been more involved had I been in the States.

Due to my limitations with the school system, Carlos took care of much of the activities and correspondence or meetings. Often, I didn't really know what was going on or I had to wait until Carlos translated for me. I felt that should have been my role and it really pulled at my self-confidence strings.

Another factor in my discomfort was that the other mothers

at the school seemed to come from wealthy households and didn't work. I always felt like the other women showed up to school in full makeup and jewelry or with a nanny and I was usually in my favorite workout gear, heading to the gym before work. I had no time or desire to chit-chat, I just wanted to drop off my kids and go. Eventually, I stopped participating in school activities. I came to resent my decision to not put my kids in English-speaking schools, but it was too late and we were priced out of the best schools. I had to constantly remind myself of the goal to help my children be fully bilingual and know both of their cultures, which was not always easy for me.

Unfortunately, before and during my relocation, I didn't have the luxury of learning firsthand what to do and what not to do to interact in business and socially on the island, and I made many mistakes. A girl from the Northeast with a strong personality who had worked in a corporate atmosphere before relocating was in for a ride. Little did I know how that would harm me and my relationships in the future, especially in business.

These experiences were factors in my future decision to become certified as a cultural trainer. Shortly after working in the clinic, the owner approached me with a request she had received from a company in the United States. They were looking for a therapist who was willing to fly to Miami to be trained through "Living & Working in Puerto Rico" seminars as a cultural trainer to work with relocating corporate employees and their families. They also had programs just for spouses and children, which excited me. Where had these been when I relocated?

So, with encouragement from Carlos, I flew to Florida and came back as the only "certified" cultural trainer on the island. I felt a great need to help others, especially the spouses. My frustrations and hardships could have been greatly minimized had I been supported and given important cultural information I had taught in the training sessions. This experience motivated me to open my own consulting business and private practice, which I was very proud of.

My mission then became to help and support other families relocating to the island. My own experience of relocating as a "trailing spouse," pregnant mother, and an American allowed me to attend clients in therapy with their challenges and concerns about their re-location.

Eventually, I was recognized for my work and interviewed by the *Caribbean Business Magazine* on three occasions, for the issues of "Culture Shock Caribbean" (March 2006), "Most Powerful Business Women" (July 2006), and "Companies in Motion" (January 2007).

I believe that if I had received some cultural training of my own, my marriage and my mental state would have suffered less during this transition. Would I have drank less? I'm not sure, but I seemed to be in a constant struggle with my self-esteem and identity. So, during this time of professional recognition, I felt like a new woman—empowered and confident.

Unfortunately, this feeling didn't carry over at home and in the community. There was the constant reminder at every turn that I was a foreigner. Everything was in Spanish, which I did not understand fully yet. I constantly had to rely on Carlos, and I detested the fact that I needed to depend on someone to live day to day in my own home or environment.

Carlos had a demanding job, as most corporate workers do. This left me alone with the kids much of the time. I became resentful with my neediness and inability to get around and understand things on my own. A simple task like going to a new doctor or store ended with me pulling over on the side of the road or highway because I couldn't understand the signs, sometimes with a screaming child in the car seat. Back then there was no GPS, and Hurricane George destroyed most road signs, and many were never replaced. I was used to the orderly structure of the mainland. On the island there was often no street numbering and, worse, some streets had three different names that I couldn't pronounce.

Even at family gatherings—and I loved my in-laws and they loved me—I felt like an intruder. Often when I entered the room while they were talking or laughing and doing what was natural for them in their language, they would frequently have to switch to English to include me. Sometimes they would unintentionally forget, which left me clueless. I got good at "tuning out" and isolating in my own world. Often my answer was to escape with a drink to ease my discomfort or upset. Nobody knows this feeling of solitude unless they actually experience it. I also got good at hiding it and pretending that I was fine.

Luckily, Carlos always agreed to take yearly family trips to Connecticut at Christmas. This allowed my children to be surrounded by my family and to experience snow and even a ski trip. The traditional dishes my mom made during the holidays were the best part, which I have always repeated while in Puerto Rico to carry on the tradition of her cooking.

It was difficult for me to express my internal pain to Carlos. On the outside, it appeared we had everything we needed: a beautiful family, he had a good job, I was working, nice cars. But those things were superficial and my soul was screaming with sadness. How could he empathize if even I didn't really understand it? The chipping away of my self-esteem and sense of who I was continued to wear on me. I often felt my spouse may have longed for the independent single woman he met in Florida, but she seemed lost. I longed for her many times, too. The number one rule in recovery is to avoid resentments, and boy, did I seem to be piling them on. Sadly, the strong independent woman I had regained after my first marriage was now slowly fading again. As a way to have some sense of control over my life, I became focused with a vengeance on my looks, labeling and making photo albums, working out, cooking and entertaining.

Even with my intention of a total immersion plan in Puerto Rico, I was still only partially fluent in Spanish. I was never afraid to speak, just limited in the vocabulary and tenses. With the children and work, I stopped taking classes and hit a wall with my ability to speak the language. My job allowed me to speak English all day with my clients in the clinic, which allowed for me to finally feel comfortable.

After about a year on the island, I had an exciting encounter while grocery shopping one day. I encountered another American woman speaking English to her kids. I was like a lost puppy dog— I immediately wanted to get to know her. We started chatting like old friends, and she told me about a club she was in, the Newcomers Club of Puerto Rico. I was shocked that I didn't know about this club. *You mean there are others like me on the island?!*

After exchanging information, I went home excited about my new friend. Almost immediately, I became a member and attended one of their monthly luncheons, where I met a few women I liked and started to feel a connection with and relief from my loneliness. They had a monthly newsletter and cultural events like 4th of July picnics and BBQs. These gatherings reminded me of my upbringing in the Northeast. I also received a members' directory, which had contact information of recommended doctors and resources. I felt like I had hit the jackpot!

THE SPLIT

To the outside world, we may have appeared as the perfect family. Sadly, inside was a different reality. Days ran into nights and the arguing escalated. I'm not sure how or when the decision happened, as I look back now and try to recapture the feelings and moments, it seems like a blur or another family's movie. It was a very difficult decision for both of us and a painful time in my life.

Nonetheless, there we were, with our sadness, loneliness, disappointment, and anger. Things didn't appear to improve and my drinking didn't help matters for either of us. It's curious to me now that I ever found the strength or made a decision to separate or leave the marriage. I loved my husband very much and never looked elsewhere in the ten years we were married. He was my everything, my sober white knight, whom I was very proud of. Unfortunately, I was of the mindset that just because a person didn't drink often or wasn't an alcoholic, they were better than me. Do I have regrets? I suppose I have many and I have played them all out thousands of times. After sobriety, I learned, in the program, to not regret the past nor wish to shut the door on it. I do know that I could not continue with the way I was living or feeling. I could not or did not want to get sober at that point. I regret many things, but I'll never regret having the courage to get sober and find myself again. At some point during my recovery, I had to forgive myself and my ex and learn to move forward as a kind and sober person, with my head up and to live with my choices.

Our ten-year anniversary was approaching amid all these sad and complicated emotions. But, we decided to go through with a celebration to mark this special event. With heavy hearts, we did what we thought was the "correct" thing and had a party, including screening videos of our engagement and marriage. We drank champagne and danced with all our family and friends. I knew we both felt that weight in our hearts. But just as we always did, we put on a good show! It wasn't until a few months later that we finally decided to talk, as the arguing and subsequent silences had become too much for us both. My drinking had increased and became a center of many discussions, too. At one point I thought maybe I should try again to stop drinking, once and for all. But, how? We were always either entertaining or going to a party.

I finally found the courage one day to approach Carlos.

"I'd like to try to stop drinking. Do you think we could not have any alcohol in the house, to help me get started?"

"It's your problem, not mine," he retorted. I believe he was exhausted with me and my many previous attempts.

It was then that I realized the reality and pain of what I was living. I was silently begging to be helped and expressing it verbally took a lot for me. Why was the idea of putting me in a treatment center never mentioned?! At first, I didn't want to stop drinking, and then I couldn't stop drinking. I was in hell and couldn't find my way out. My ego didn't allow for me to admit defeat after I had been trying so hard for the entire marriage. The children were still young and I wasn't sure I knew what to expect of any different way of life. I was scared to death of any kind of separation or change. I did know that I couldn't continue the way things were.

In a final attempt to regain some normalcy, we went on a family trip to Connecticut with the kids. We both made efforts to rekindle what had been lost. Unfortunately, the heaviness of our individual pain weighed on us both.

Once we returned to Puerto Rico with the arguing continuing, we had our first real discussion on what we wanted to do. That night was a difficult one, which would ultimately change both of our lives. We started sleeping in separate bedrooms, and finally, we had the talk with the children, which was heartbreaking to all of us. The kids were seven and ten. Jessica took it harder, as she was older and had more of a grasp on what was happening. The next step was for Carlos to move out of the home we had made together over the past decade. That day, my world slowly came crashing down, as it did for all of us.

With no one monitoring my drinking, not having the children with me all the time allowed me to drink more freely, and it became my only relief from my pain, fear, and suffering. I became angry and bitter, which led to me drinking to black out as often as I could. *Oh… What had we done?* The decision and damage done was haunting me in every part of my body and soul. Neither of us had made any attempt at that point to save the marriage.

Living on the island alone in my huge house we had built was more than I could bear. I felt like somebody had cut my arms and legs off… I didn't know how to live or what to do. I had no sense of who I was, and the holidays were coming up. Where would I spend them, and what would I do now? The kids were used to large family gatherings and me cooking for everybody. I knew I couldn't keep them from their usual traditions. Therefore, I allowed them to be with Carlos and his family during the first holiday after our separation. That first holiday was excruciatingly painful. I cried most of the night.

The idea of me returning alone to Connecticut was not appealing. *How could I go home without my family, and face everybody?* My shame and depression returned with a vengeance. That was not an option. I'm not sure why my family didn't seem to understand my torment and pain. Maybe I didn't show it, or I pretended I was okay. But I wasn't. I wanted to be rescued and hugged and told all would be well. Instead, I suffered in silence.

I knew I couldn't handle questions that I wouldn't have answers to. I also wanted to be near my children even if I couldn't be with them. So, when they weren't home I cried, drank, and slipped further into the abyss.

One day the children were at home with me, and I had been so depressed and panicked that I hid in the kitchen pantry, crying. I finally told the children to call their father to pick them up. I was screaming for help from the inside out. Carlos picked them up and I was still alone with my grief and confusion about what was happening to me. I secretly had wanted to be admitted to a hospital as I couldn't function or take care of myself or the kids. Carlos never asked me if I was okay. *Do you need help? Why are you holed up in the pantry?* Instead, Carlos was so angry with me, and I got the silent treatment.

Carlos seemed to completely change shortly after the separation, and he started dating. This was a man I seemed to no longer recognize and it sent me over the edge with rage and sadness. Why wasn't he also in pain and suffering? *Did I ever really know you? How could you do this so soon and in front of my babies? Don't you see I am dying here?*

I couldn't contain myself or my emotions during this time. I became like a lioness, which any mother can relate to. The constant drinking left me fragile and with a weak and damaged filter on how I spoke or behaved. I was out of my mind with a dark sense of loss, grief, and disorientation. *Where do I go? I have no friends here. How is it possible that I'm now being replaced so quickly?*

During this bleak time I became friends with a French woman from my children's school, a divorced mom like me with a couple of kids and about the same age. She was a hoot—she drank like a sailor and never seemed to get drunk. I secretly thought she must have a wooden leg where she stashed the booze. I tried to keep up with her but I was a light-weight black-out drinker by that point. But we drank and smoked together and I found a thread of hope in a new friendship during my tragedy.

She finally convinced me to go out as a single woman for the first time in over twelve years. It was a devastating experience for me, I didn't enjoy going out unless I was sedated with drinks. Then, of course I changed and became a person I didn't like at all. It was a vicious cycle. This behavior left a wake of many amends to be made—now I was the person I couldn't recognize and my anger at my losses was debilitating.

My initial solo venturing out proved dangerous. I had always had a cushion with my drinking, because Carlos would help me or care for me and the kids if I drank too much, which was every time we went out. At my first unaccompanied Christmas party I almost lost my reputation and my life after drinking all night. I totaled my car, and had no idea until the next day. Luckily, one of my coworkers took care of me and brought me home. I soon learned that I wasn't safe or fit to be out in public the way I drank. Therefore, I became an isolated drinker when the kids weren't home. We co-parented, but they seemed to be with their dad more often, as he had more family events and support than I did, not to mention that I also didn't feel fit to have them around all the time either.

I knew I couldn't stay in the home where we had raised our children. The sadness in the house and ghosts in the walls were slowly eating away at me. Another deciding factor was that Carlos's new girlfriend lived a block away from our home. I couldn't stand being there another day. The memories and pain of what our lives had become was too much.

I began to look for a place to live for me and the kids. I wasn't working full time and I was still financially dependent on Carlos. Part of my search was filled with the dread that I would still be dependent on him. Carlos was living with his mother. At least he had someone to help with the kids when he had them and they had some sense of normalcy with their abuela. I was alone and desperate for some sanity.

HOWLING BEHIND CEMENT WALLS

Time passed. I inhabited this dark, altered state of my being, and I found this existence more excruciating each day.

On one of those dark days I awoke and tried to get the strength to get out of my large, lonely bed, but I could not. Exercise had become my form of self-medication and it was the first time I couldn't seem to get up and go to the gym. Even with my worst hangover or depression, I always seemed to make it to the gym, which made me feel better. *Why go to the gym? For what? Why even get up?*

The master bedroom was huge, enclosed by thick cement walls. There I was, in my empty king-size bed, surrounded by these walls I never seemed to notice before. I could have sworn they were moving in on me. I felt like I was in a prison. I missed my old life and I missed my husband dreadfully.

This was not a coherent thought. You see, I missed him and despised him at the same time. *How could he not have fought for us?* Even though it wasn't just his responsibility, I wondered why he didn't see how sick I was and try to help me, his wife for over a decade, the mother of his children? *How could he have moved on with his life and another woman so easily and quickly, while I was slowly spiraling out of control with grief?*

I couldn't understand what was happening to me. It was so improbable that I was being replaced. I thought I always had things under control. But we both had grown bitter and angry with each other and the children were suffering, too. We once had a love story that I was so proud of. Now, it was one I could only dream about.

Seeing the man I had loved and admired for so long change and the two of us speaking to each other and doing the things we were doing destroyed my last ounce of "normal" and my dream of growing old together. There was no I... I had only known we. I was completely lost. Somehow, I slowly slid off the bed onto the floor. I was still unable to stand or know what to do next. Nothing made sense anymore. I transcended into another reality of disorientation and grief, slowly drowning in my own pain. I started to sob. Sitting on the floor, clinging to the bed like a life preserver, I wished for some kind of relief.

As I sobbed uncontrollably for hours, I became frightened. The room I knew so well for over ten years had become my prison cell. Cold, dark, and empty. I heard a faint noise. I couldn't separate reality from delusion anymore. *Was I really hearing this? What was that sound?*

It didn't sound human to me, and it came from so far away. Painful and sad at the same time. I attempted to get my bearings and as I imagined the image of a wolf howling in pain it grew louder! I thought I could see this creature through swollen-shut eyes.

So, now I am going crazy? Seeing animals through closed eyes? Where is that sound coming from? Doesn't anybody hear that poor animal in pain? Still on the floor fading in and out of reality, I grasped the side of the bed and buried my face in the sheets. It seemed an eternity before I was able to lift my head. I tried to open at least one eye to get a grip on my surroundings. My throat burned with pain.

Then… *Oh my God… That sound is you, Lynn!*

That howling and screaming was coming from me all along and had been for hours. Like a lone wolf separated from the pack, howling for help. I had lost my voice, my soul, and any sense of reality that morning. Nothing would ever be the same.

Hours later I found the strength to go to the bathroom and look in the mirror. The face looking back was not mine—she looked old, worn, and full of fear. That day I found the courage to reach out for help. With a voice hoarse from howling, I attempted a call for an emergency appointment with a psychiatrist I knew. I had referred several patients to him in the past and he knew me well. Once his secretary heard my desperation, she told me to come in immediately.

I cried and mumbled incoherently throughout the entire session. I'm not quite sure how I got there or what I said. Looking back, I never should have driven and I should have been brought to a hospital. Even though I was totally sober, I was drunk with desperation and panic. Why this doctor did not hospitalize me baffles me to this day. Why no one helped me during this dark time confuses me. Could I have been that good at hiding my pain? How could I have pretended so well?

The doctor simply suggested a prescription for an antidepressant. No therapy, just medication. At that moment I thought, Well, at least *somebody* can see I'm not doing well. Maybe medication was the answer to my misery. Good old Western medicine. I hadn't been medicated before yet it brought relief to my suffering, like some sense of security that there was a solution and reason for why I was completely broken and apparently delusional. The wolf!

Ahhhh… I'm depressed, that's what's happening.

By end of the session I confessed that I had thought about ending my life or checking myself in somewhere. I told him that I couldn't stand another day in my own skin and that I couldn't function properly. But I wasn't hospitalized, although I denied any kind of plan at the time.

To be fair, I wasn't totally honest with him about how severe my drinking had become. Of course alcohol is a depressant, like adding fuel to the fire. So, I was counting on the pills to help me to figure things out and get better.

I started on the medication and felt somewhat better. A few weeks passed and I continued to drink, despite the recommendation in the directions not to. I wasn't ready to live life on sober terms, even with the medication. My isolation was daunting and began to totally suffocate me.

Finally, with no real relief, I returned to the doctor once again. This time I was honest about my drinking and my inability to stop. I asked him if he could give me something to help me stop the cravings for alcohol, along with the antidepressant that he had prescribed me.

What shocks me now is that a medical doctor, knowing my addiction history and struggle with depression, did not recommend a treatment facility or twelve-step program. On my own, it honestly never occurred to me to return to recovery or go to a treatment program. First, there were no facilities in Puerto Rico in English, as

I had researched this at one point for an American patient of mine. So, even if I had wanted to go, or was referred, where would I go?

I had become delusional and believed my addiction was not that bad. Of course, the additional pill that he gave me for drinking did nothing, as I knew that whenever I wanted to get drunk, I would just not take the pill.

Eventually, I found a new place to live. Downsizing from a beautiful huge home to a condominium was a challenge. After weeks of searching and becoming disheartened, here was a place that just might be doable for me. The first issue was that I needed to purchase it quickly, because the owner was giving me a good deal. The second issue was that I was still legally married.

Seeing no hope or attempt to rescue our marriage, I pushed to get to the lawyer and sign the paperwork. I wanted to purchase something on my own, not while married. I had never been the sole owner of my own place. This was a huge step for me. The closing process, which should have been one of excitement and a show of courage left me with a severe migraine and panic attack. I had no idea about most of what I was signing and I had nobody there to help me. Everything was in Spanish and I was totally overwhelmed and terrified.

By the time I arrived at my mother-in-law's to pick up the kids, I was exhausted. She put me in a bedroom and I was there for a long time crying, and moaning from my throbbing migraine. I vaguely remember my daughter coming in and crawling in bed with me, telling me everything would be okay and that she loved me. She was so sweet and had no idea of what was ahead, she had rarely seen me so vulnerable.

As I was in no condition to care of the kids, I left them with their abuela and somehow drove home. When I got there I was vomiting from the pain and heartache and it was all I could do to crawl into bed with an ice pack.

The next day I went to the doctor for more pain medicine for the migraines. Later I discovered they were stress-related. I wasn't supposed to drink on these pain killers, either. But when the pain eventually subsided, I started again. The combination was lethal and as I continued to drink and black out, and my emotions and health spiraled downward.

I tried to get the kids excited about the new place, and initially they were. It was an empty condo with no air conditioning units, lighting, or landscaping—I was the first owner. The task of choosing and paying for fixtures was overwhelming.

Moving out of my home, packing up memories and pictures, seemed more than I could bear. I picked my wedding album and it felt like another lifetime to me. I couldn't find the strength to take it with me. So, there it remained, in the garage with other items I chose to leave behind. This is the part of my journey that absolutely saddens and sickens me. As I recall the memories it seems like someone else's life. *How and why did we do this? Why was there no intervention?*

START OF RECOVERY

Somehow, I managed to continue working and providing services in therapy and cultural training programs. This gave me a sense of purpose and normalcy that I believe kept me alive.

As I always say, the Universe has a sense of timing and humor.

One day I received a call from a new client. She had found me on the Newcomers Club of Puerto Rico website where I was listed as a resource.

Carrie entered the room and I liked her immediately. Unbeknownst to me, my life would start to take a profound shift that day. She was an American, recently transferred to Puerto Rico with her spouse and newborn baby. Her initial consult was for cultural challenges and marital issues.

Carrie was a wonderful client and a beautiful messenger in my life. During our sessions, she revealed that she had been in recovery for many years. Of course, I knew the program well, as it had saved my life over a decade ago in Miami, Florida. I hadn't thought of returning to this program for years. Now, I was relieved to hear her story. In one of our sessions, I felt comfortable enough to ask her where the meetings were held, for "another client," of course. I kept the information in my agenda book for another few weeks. Carrie gave me hope and she was a breath of fresh air in my life. I liked her and wished she weren't my client so that we could be friends. I looked forward to our sessions, which made me feel somehow safe and grounded again, peaceful. I identified with her story and longed for her sobriety. As I worked with her, I was impressed and motivated by her strength, hope, and solutions to remain sober despite her challenges. My angel of a client had sparked hope in me again. To this day I am grateful for her. Years after I stopped seeing her in therapy, I would see her at a meeting, and we became friends and are to this day.

These encounters inspired me to return to twelve-step meetings after more than a decade. My ability to work and function professionally always gave me the false illusion that I was okay. Deep down, I knew that wasn't true. I was making mistakes with my clients like missing appointments and overbooking, and I was irritable with my staff.

Miraculously, there I was, standing outside the meeting location. I hesitated, and took a detour to a corner restaurant and had lunch and tried to convince myself that I didn't need to go back to those damn meetings and people. Yet somehow I found my way to the noon meeting near the Caribe Hilton Hotel, at "The Serenity Room." This later became the place I called my home group and saved my life and my sanity once again. There I found a new family and friends that loved me unconditionally and helped me regain my sobriety, soul, and dignity.

Although the twelve-step recovery program helped restore my sobriety, I was still full of rage and resentment. I could barely maintain my composure for having to be there, while my ex was moving on and now engaged.

Going back to when I had first come in at almost thirty years old was the only way that I knew in my heart would save me again. But leaving behind my two loves—alcohol and cigarettes—was a source of constant pain and dependency I didn't want to part with. Isolation and blackouts had become my source of comfort. The group listened to my emotional venom with tenderness and without judgment.

I did this for some time, spilling over with anger and complaining or accusing Carlos, Puerto Rico, the lack of street signs, chickens roaming free, or anywhere else I could deflect my rage. Reluctantly, I returned to the rooms of recovery and once again picked up a chip to surrender, and found myself a sponsor.

One day I confessed to my sponsor, Mindy, that I really wanted to find a way to poison and kill the damn coqui frogs that were blasting their chirping all night. In my insomnia, I had even gone online and

Googled how to do it. We still laugh about it and I'm happy to report that I did not act on these thoughts or poison any of the beautiful coqui frogs of Puerto Rico. Eventually, my irritability subsided and I made peace with nature, their chirping, and my irrational desires.

I had no idea how severe my detox would be from withdrawals this time around. The first few nights in sobriety I felt severe itching all over my body. I freaked out and thought my new bed must have bed bugs. I sat up all night checking (finding nothing) and went to the store the next day and bought a protective mattress cover.

I realized much later that I was in withdrawal. I had trouble focusing, sleeping, and controlling all my emotions. During this entire nightmare, Mindy would listen gently and always end with "I love you." These were words I longed for in the depths of my solitude. She would encourage me to go out with the group after meetings, but I detested this idea of going out without drinking. I had become an isolator and the idea of being with all these strangers and their loud behavior was not appealing at all. This was such a transformation from who I once was—a socialite, loving dressing up and going out dancing. But without alcohol, I simply wasn't interested.

Eventually, with her loving coaxing, I joined them one evening for dinner. The people in the group made me cringe from their happiness and noisiness. I had been alone for so long that this kind of stimulation seemed to hurt all over. I certainly didn't have any intentions of doing that again!

My sponsor gently continued to persuade me and soon we were doing breakfast, dinner, and other events. Eventually I became part of this new family and I started to feel as if I had a home and friends who welcomed me with open arms.

My struggle did not end, though. Dealing with Carlos and the kids was a huge emotional challenge. I had a difficult time witnessing the man I was married to for so long suddenly with another woman and my kids, like a new family. Not to mention their sleepovers at her house (on the floor of the same room they slept in), which made me mad like a woman on fire. I felt the children were such innocents and should be allowed to grieve our family separation before starting another so soon. Their dad didn't agree. It crushed me and also encouraged me to stay sober. I somehow felt he was my property and those were certainly my children... I birthed, loved, and cared for them. No woman was going to replace me! I felt like a wounded and trapped animal.

In the early years of sobriety my emotions were unstable. I felt like I was being unfairly tested and was constantly angry with my situation. Some say you get on a "pink cloud" at the beginning of sobriety. *Hell, no!* Thunderous black clouds tortured me daily.

With the help of the meetings, my sponsor, and my will to change, I was able to get sober on January 2, 2009. I started to feel my strength return.

I stayed sober for a month and a half, which was a miracle for me at that time. Then Valentine's Day arrived. This was the first Valentine's Day celebration I went through divorced and sober. So, on that special day, which Carlos and I had celebrated for the past thirteen years together, my sobriety was really put to the test. I wanted to do something with my kids, but they were with their dad and his girlfriend and her children out at the movies. *Great... a big happy Valentine's Day family event.* I detested them both!

In an effort to entertain myself that night and with no friends to go out with, I decided to take myself to the movies. *How pathetic would it be if I ran into them at the same theater. I would surely have to kill myself.* So, I ventured to a theater some distance away, that wasn't in a nice area or near my home, but I was sure nobody would see me there. I sat through *Benjamin Button* with Brad Pitt, the most depressing movie I could have watched, and a sad love story, too. After crying through almost the entire movie, I left in even worse spirits.

With tears in my eyes and bad popcorn in my stomach, I left the dirty theater and parking lot. Immediately, my restlessness and aching heart started to kick in. The idea that I was in a disgusting theater on Valentine's Day, alone, became too much. *Who can do this sober?* In the car my thoughts turned to a way to make it all better: a drink. *Yes, a good bottle of wine, cigarettes, and then a blackout is what I need.*

I reached out to my sponsor and she didn't answer her phone. I called another fellow member and they didn't answer either. So, then the internal chatter started: *What a joke these people are. The meetings are a waste of my time. Blah, blah, blah.*

I love humor, so when I relive this part of my journey, I like to say that I was a girl who loved bananas!

"What?" you ask? "Bananas? I don't understand, Lynn."

Well, "bananas" was my code word to say that I needed to go to the grocery story to get something healthy. Then, on the sly, I would slide past the wine area and pick up a bottle of Pinot Grigio, which led to a pack of Marlboro Lights. All along with the intention of getting bananas!

So that is exactly what went down. Once I entered the store that Valentine's Day, there was no hesitation. Then I raced home and couldn't open that wine fast enough. In my mind it was only a month and a half… no big deal!

Upon that first sip I felt like I was home and had absolutely no regrets. *Happy Freaking Valentine's Day, girlfriend. We are going down.*

The next morning I awoke for the first time in a month and a half to a hangover and the familiar self-loathing once again. *What have I done?* I still was alone, now just with a hangover and cigarette mouth. I hated cigarettes, too! Ugh.

I picked up the phone and called my sponsor. She was a tough bird, thirty years sober and didn't coddle me at all. She was kind of nasty if I remember correctly. Something about "So, how did that work for you?" *Bitch*, I thought.

That response turned out to be the fuel I needed. An I'll-show-her kind of attitude. I returned to a meeting that day and picked up another chip to start my recovery once again. The only thing my new family said was "welcome back" and again without judgment.

Shortly after that, I found a different sponsor that I liked. She's still my sponsor today. I love her for being in my life, loving me when I could not love myself, and guiding me through the steps. We continue our step work all these years later.

That was the beginning of my journey to find out what kind of sober woman I could be. February 15, 2019 marked twelve years sober for me. I had struggled being with my own company for so long and always seemed to need a partner. I feared and loathed being alone. Little did I know that I would enjoy having an intense love affair with myself for the next twelve years. That was just one gift of many of the promises in sobriety I had not counted on.

If only you don't drink... the pain will pass.

THE AWAKENING

Along my path of sobriety, I found many hidden strengths and desires I never knew I had or wanted. I discovered I was an intuitive psychotherapist, a dynamic speaker, and an entrepreneur. I felt confident I could help clients with my new-found abilities.

An additional revelation was the beautiful gift buried inside, and desire to be a compassionate sacred healer. I always knew I wanted to help people in a different "holistic" way, but I never knew what path I would venture on to do that.

They say when the student is ready, the teacher appears. One day during the time I was working as a Reiki Master teacher, a friend introduced me to a wonderful spiritually gifted man to provide a "house cleansing" for me.

During his many hours at my home we got to know each other well, and he confided that he was a sacred healer, too. My interest was piqued. We spoke in length more about this method of energy healing, my recent trainings as a healer, and my desires to keep evolving as an energy healer.

I knew I had to receive a healing from him and asked for a personal session as soon as possible. Shortly after our meeting I drove to San Lorenzo to his office for my first experience on the healing table with him.

Floating off the table, all I could say was "I don't know what just happened, but I want to learn what you just did." That was the beginning of my attending retreats, seminars and being initiated as a sacred healer, in which I take great pride and joy.

Initially, I went through extensive training as a Reiki Master Teacher, then flew to Arizona and studied Cranial Sacral Therapy, then Pranic Healing and finally my current method, providing "Sacred Healing through the Paramita Path." To me it is the highest form of energy healing and love.

During my divorce and my experience as a "patient," I experienced first-hand the "Western medicine" way of diagnosing and medicating. Now, for some people this may be the last resort and necessary. I'm not a medical doctor nor do I convince people to go on or off medication if they are needed. It is a personal decision, which I respect either way.

"Sacred Healing" is a healing technique based on divine Love that opens your energy portals and allows you to heal at very deep levels. In sacred healing, you receive a powerful healing attunement that will open your energy channels to heal and awaken your heart. It also allows you to remember who you are. The results in my patients are a fast and easy healing with their life struggles or addictions. This is not to say that another healing method isn't effective. Everybody finds and studies what they need at any given time, which I respect.

After years of research, I now compliment my private practice with cognitive and behavioral therapy, energy healing, sacred oils accompanied by special quartzes, crystals, and meditations. I find this greatly complements psychotherapy and expedites the healing process of the mind, body, and soul.

In Sacred Healing, the powerful healing functions of quartzes and seashells are garnered to render a healing that is deep and far-reaching. A request is made during the session for the healing of any karma you may have with illness so that you may take full advantage of the energy healing that follows.

However, the most important element of Sacred Healing is its complete reliance and surrender to Divine Love. The sacred healer who transmits the healing is an instrument through which the Light of Pure Love can come through and heal. Sacred healing can be transmitted to you in person or from a distance.

Awakening
is not changing who you are,
but discarding who you are not.

DEEPAK CHOPRA

EPILOGUE

It took me years to find the courage to write my story. Finding that bravery has allowed me to find my hidden strengths and joy. I also hope my story can serve by touching someone's life. It might help to learn about another's journey in *recovery, depression, relocation, divorce* and *family loss*. All of these different challenges have allowed for me to mend the broken pieces and recreate myself to be better than ever.

Now, getting sober was not an easy task and I had many slips and obstacles to overcome. Dealing with fear of financial instability, developing a business on an island and culture that are not my own, healing wounds with myself, my ex-husband, and family were often daunting tasks.

They still can be in some respects, but I thankfully have a tool box of solutions to deal with anything that comes my way. As long as I remember it is always me and not anything else that is the problem, I can resolve any situation. Trust in some higher source other than yourself... I choose to use the term The Divine., clean your house, and most of all, "Don't drink!" *Show up, suit up, and step up!*

By doing my step work I was encouraged to own my role in my marriage, which allowed for me to forgive and come full circle. I mostly had to forgive my own self, which I had treated so harshly over the years. I carried a lot of guilt about my children being greatly affected by the divorce, as we all were. This weighed heavily on my parenting style and co-dependency. In the beginning, I went to extremes to assure they were happy and I gave them everything they wanted. Many times I believe I went too far with my guilt.

It took years before I felt grounded and proud to change how I parented and love them without any guilt or anger. I found balance in saying "no" and enforcing rules that I couldn't before. That shift didn't come without resistance, anger, and more guilt.

The twelve-step recovery program allows for solutions to live a life of making amends and cleaning your side of the street with what damage you may have caused another person.

I made amends the best I could with people I had hurt; I was frightened that I would be rejected, attacked, or dismissed. In some cases I was, or my attempts via letters I sent were ignored. My sponsor taught me that making amends doesn't mean you'll get a standing ovation or a pat on the back. You do it for your peace of mind and serenity. Another protective tool in your path of sobriety.

I also was able to heal my relationship with Carlos, which I put great effort into. Resentments are dangerous to a recovering person, and I knew better to have any lingering poison in my head. With time, I was able to manage celebrating holiday dinners at my house together as a family and I invited him. This is a gift of the program and of being a sober person.

You may ask how I do it. I say this is the behavior of a healed heart, clear mind, and sobriety. Why not?

I will always have a love in my heart for my children's father, and I am grateful for all the lessons he has allowed me to learn along my journey. I know that we both would help each other in any way we might need. This is yet another blessing of the program and working through the steps. I have made several attempts at verbal amends with him. Now I express myself through my actions.

My children say they never really remember me being drunk, and I tried my best to hide that part of me when I was with them. I was a binge night-time weekend-warrior drinker, often in isolation rather than in public.

Sobriety has also enabled me to be present for the deaths of my parents, which were devastating events.

Years ago, when Mom was ill, I had started working in the healing world. I had become certified as a Reiki master teacher at that time. I flew home the day she was put in hospice to be there for her passing. I am clear that she waited for all her children to be there before she transitioned.

I had the privilege to be present and love her in the end the best I knew how. I was able to crawl in the hospice bed with her and give her healing treatment for fear and transitioning before she passed. Mom left while in my arms, with one hand on her heart and the other on her crown radiating healing love and light during her process. For the child who gave her the most grief, it gave me comfort to think I made some kind of amends that day.

Mom was a beautiful, brave woman and she was absolutely terrified to leave the family she loved so much. She was a loving mother in her own way, with a complex personality. Deep conversations about intimate things were never discussed, and so I had to make them up as I went through life as a teen and young adult. But family was everything to her and in the end we were all there and I know she felt the loving presence of each of us.

Dad passed shortly after Mom did, from stomach cancer. During that time I had the opportunity to make verbal amends with him, just as I had done with my mother on a previous visit. When I was a kid, Dad had a harsh temperament that would occasionally become physical with me as well as verbal. I was often afraid of him, which was not the type of relationship I wanted to have. Following the program guidelines and my sponsor's encouragement has allowed me to free my heart from any remorse I may have had of regrets or resentments. I did the best I could, as we all do with what we know at any given time.

Thankfully, I have had the honor of having a love affair with myself for these sober years every day, no matter what has transpired. I have learned to be gentle, kind and forgiving of myself. I am blessed to own my own home, to be a loving, kind mother, ex-spouse, and sister if my siblings desire. I also am proud to be of service to my clients, inspiring strength and hope with my experiences as a sober woman with dignity.

When I feel overwhelmed with my emotions or life, I try to pick up the phone, be of service, or get to a meeting. If I can get out of my own way and work with others and be grateful, things always seem to turn out the way they should.

Today I am proud to say that after much struggle I finally found my truth. As my life cleared I lost the fear of sharing my story. My hope is that this book may have inspired anyone struggling with addiction, divorce, depression, relocation, or just feeling lost. Sharing my story has helped me to heal. The truth shall set you free!

The spiritual journey
is the unlearning of fear
and the acceptance of love.

MARIANNE WILLIAMSON

I wish for you, and for all of those who suffer today at the hands of some addiction, that you find your way to enjoy the peace and amazing life that I have found for myself in recovery. There is always a way out. Owning our journey is a gift we should embrace.

Know that you have all the power you need to turn your life around with just one step. My hopes and dreams continue and I try to live one day at a time until they manifest!

Sobriety allows for unlimited possibilities. Remember, there are **THREE** things we must do to be successful throughout our walk in that gratifying road of recovery:

- Accept your truth
- Get to the start of that road
- Walk it without worries of finding a finish line

For recovery will always be a journey, not a destination.

"No matter how much people recognize you, or how popular you are with them, you will be unhappy unless you acknowledge yourself. True recognition does not only come from those around you or the world. It comes when you recognize and love yourself."

Iᴌᴄʜɪ Lᴇᴇ, *Living Tao: Timeless Principles for Everyday Enlightenment*

What's next for me...

Much love, light, and joy to you and your journey.

THE WOLF

Wolf power or wolves as spirit animals point to an appetite for freedom and living life powerfully, guided by instincts. When a wolf manifests its presence as a guide in your life, it could be a call to live your life more freely, to bring the intensity of passion in your everyday endeavors.

Wolves are wild animals that are not easily domesticated and when they appear as spirit guides, they could be an invitation to look at what supports your authentic self and the true expression of yourself. The wolf totem is a reminder to keep your spirit alive and trust your instincts to find the way that will best suit you.

A symbol of freedom and wisdom, the wolf often appears to guide your journey of self-discovery.

ACKNOWLEDGEMENTS

First and foremost, I want to express my deepest gratitude to my dear friend, author Pilar Sinquemani, for her encouragement, mentoring, professional expertise, and writing/editing skills she offered to help make this book happen. Her loving encouragement and professional advice allowed for me to continue when I wanted to quit. For that I will always be thankful.

I also want to mention dear friends along the way who encouraged me to move forward, and to not look back. I met Arma Merediz, my long-time sister on the path, when I first got sober in Miami (1988). She never gave up on me. "You can do this," she would always tell me. My other sister on my life path is a very close friend Kim in Atlanta, GA. I met her years ago in Puerto Rico and we were connected from the beginning. She always says "listen to your soul voice... you got this!"

To the loves of my life, my children: Jessica and Peter. They have inspired me to be a better person, mother, and role model. I love them to the moon and back, and am proud to be their mom. I am grateful that their father and I were able to heal our wounds and forge a mutual friendship.

The wound is the place where the light enters you.

RUMI

HOWLING BEHIND CEMENT WALLS
by Lynn Stravecky
was printed in the United States of America
on September 2021.

Made in United States
North Haven, CT
20 October 2021